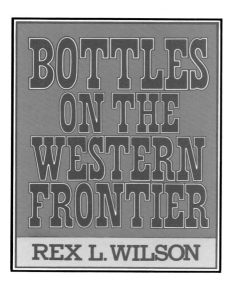

BOTTLES ON THE WESTERN FRONTIER

REX L. WILSON

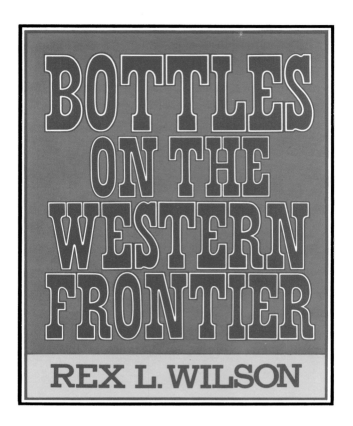

BOTTLES ON THE WESTERN FRONTIER

REX L. WILSON

Edited by Edward Staski

Published by
THE UNIVERSITY OF ARIZONA PRESS
Tucson, Arizona
in collaboration with
SOUTHWEST PARKS AND MONUMENTS ASSOCIATION

About the Author

For nearly 20 years Rex Wilson kept directly involved with the management of archaeological salvage programs in the United States. As senior archaeologist in the Department of the Interior he, before coming to the National Trust on a special two-year assignment in 1979, served as Departmental Consulting Archaeologist for the Department of the Interior and as Chief of Interagency Archaeological Services in the National Park Service. Between 1958 and 1962 Mr. Wilson was archaeologist at Fort Union National Monument and Museum Curator at Fort Laramie National Historic Site.

THE UNIVERSITY OF ARIZONA PRESS

This book was set in 11/12 and 9/10 pt. V-I-P Memphis.
Copyright © 1981
The Arizona Board of Regents
All rights reserved
Manufactured in the U.S.A.

Library of Congress Cataloging in Publication Data

Wilson, Rex L.
  Bottles on the western frontier.

  Bibliography: p.
  1. Bottles—West (U.S.) I. Staski, Edward.
II. Title.
NK5440.B6W57   748.8'2'0973   81-11703
ISBN 0-8165-0414-8   AACR2
ISBN 0-8165-0756-2 (pbk.)

CONTENTS

Bottles on the Western Frontier is meant to be a guide and reference for the identification of bottles used on the western frontier during the second half of the nineteenth century. This study is intended primarily for the archaeologist, historian, curator, and serious collector of historic bottles; it attempts to bring together, for the first time under one cover, a representative sampling of the myriad of styles and types of bottles that were used and discarded at Fort Union, New Mexico, and Fort Laramie, Wyoming, between 1849 and 1891. It is the product of more than three years' study of thousands of bottles of all kinds that were recovered in archaeological excavations at these old army posts.

Although the almost infinite variety of the products and manufacturers represented by these bottles is little short of astounding, an explanation can be found in the people who lived on the military frontier. In essence, these nineteenth-century army posts, despite their isolation from the nuclear United States, were economic and social microcosms of the rest of the nation. Once established out west, military men, particularly officers, sent for their wives and children who eventually arrived, dusty, tired and sore, after a very long and bumpy wagon ride over the Santa Fe or Oregon Trail. Understandably, wives brought personal items in addition to pots and pans, items that normally would never have found their way to the remote west. The presence of fancy perfume vials, lotion and cologne bottles can probably be explained by the fact that these hardy souls wished to preserve some small semblance of the comparative luxuries they were accustomed to in the East. This is but one example of why it should not be surprising to find, someplace on the western frontier, practically every kind of bottle made in the United States at that time.

There were literally thousands of bottles to examine and describe, many of which were duplicates, but in order to avoid meaningless repetition I did not illustrate all of them. Many without identifying marks or special characteristics were omitted, as were those whose only distinguishing features were overall height, and size of molded lettering on the base or body.

Verification of content was greatly aided by surviving labels on specimens recovered from dry, clean, or well-drained deposits, e.g., the privy at the sutler's store, from beneath barracks floors, and from a root cellar that had collapsed and had been filled with trash at the site of the first Fort Union (1851–1861). Several beer labels were beautifully preserved because some Schlitz bottles had been incorporated within the plaster walls of an officer's house at Fort Laramie.

Identical labels consistently occurred on distinctive styles and shapes of bottles, generally confirming that all unlabeled specimens of a particular style were used for the same purpose. For example, dozens of beer labels still adhered to distinctively styled amber-colored bottles. Although such finds represent only a few of the amber-colored bottles discovered at the two posts, all bottles of that style and size were presumed to have contained beer. On the other hand, many unmarked specimens were found that may never be positively identified, their biodegradable paper labels having long since rotted away. Within this group are hundreds of different shapes and styles of bottles that probably contained patent or prescription medicines, hair oil, extracts or something to drink.

Descriptions of individual specimens cover only basic characteristics: color, neck and collar treatment, method of manufacture, markings and measurements. More specialized characteristics of fabrication, glass chemistry, or bottle closures and seals were not considered in this book.

Three categories of dates were assigned to the bottles described. Generally, closely dated specimens were those identified with their manufacturers or with the companies that packaged some kind of liquid in them. Other dates indicated represent known periods of manufacture and use. Some have been tightened through collateral research, some have been arrived at through extrapolation, and some are, frankly, best estimates. In many instances, I was unable to be more precise than sometime within the half century that Fort Union and Fort Laramie were occupied.

Because bottles were often reused in the nineteenth century, their presence as an exclusive means of dating sites is risky at best. In this instance, the sites themselves were used to date the bottles when other means were unavailable, i.e., if it was found at the first Fort Union, I dated it between 1851 and 1861, when the site was abandoned. One should also be mindful that some isolated specimens might predate or postdate either of the sites by a few years.

Additional data of general interest on late nineteenth-century bottles are offered in the appendixes. Appendix A illustrates base markings on bottles found at Fort Union. Appendix B is a tabulation of glass colors for beer bottles at both sites. Appendix C is a commentary on impressed stamps in ceramic ale bottles. Appendix D, drawn from contemporary newspapers and periodicals, is a compilation of commercial products that were packaged in glass at the time the two forts were occupied.

I extend my most sincere appreciation to the fine people with whom I worked at Fort Union National Monument and Fort Laramie National Historic Site and who kindly and patiently indulged me and my bottles between August 1958 and June 1962. Several were particularly helpful: Homer F. Hastings, former superintendent of Fort Union National Monument; George S. Cattanach Jr., who preceded me at Fort Union and who excavated most of the Fort Union bottles; and Sally Johnson Ketcham, former furnishings curator at Fort Laramie. I am singularly pleased to acknowledge Sally, who was the first to urge me to report on my bottle research and who encouraged me all the while I was writing this book. The late Newell Joyner, of the National Park Service, was highly supportive and helpful. I shall always be grateful to Nan Rickey who, as the book's first editor, added life, color, and whimsey to the text; she deserves a large share of any success that will be realized by this book.

My special thanks to James Ayres for his many helpful suggestions. With great care Jim examined each bottle at the two forts to insure the accuracy of the descriptive data included here.

Edward Staski, of the Arizona State Museum, folded in recent data developed from the archaeological salvage work in downtown Tucson and put the finishing touches on the manuscript. I am much obliged to him and to Raymond H. Thompson, Director of the Museum.

My grateful thanks to the many others who helped with the editing and with the descriptions and identifications of the bottles: Jerome E. Petsche, John D. McDermott, Richard Godfrey, Patricio G. Quintana, John Mondragon, and Martin Archuleta. And I am appreciative of the support many others provided, among them: Ray Ringenbach, the late John M. Corbett, Zorro A. Bradley, Franklin Smith, Charles C. Sharp, Douglas H. Scovill, Merrill Mattes, and the late Paul Beaubien, all of the National Park Service.

Photographs were made by Fred F. Mang Jr., of the National Park Service and by Walter and Nancy Griffith of Photographers Associated, Omaha, Nebraska. Scenes of Fort Laramie and Fort Union were photographed by Fred Mang, Jack Boucher, George S. Cattanach Jr., Homer F. Hastings, Ray Littler and myself.

Most of the information on the Anheuser-Busch Company was taken from their 1953 volume, *Making Friends Is Our Business: 100 Years of Anheuser-Busch*, and from my personal correspondence with the company. I am happy to acknowledge their contributions to this book.

I am deeply grateful to the University of Arizona Press and the Southwest Parks and Monuments Association, which collaboratively have effected publication of this book. And I extend both appreciation and apologies to those who have contributed something of substance to this book but whose names have inadvertently been omitted here.

Finally, this book represents practically everything I know about nineteenth-century bottles. It is not all I would like it to be, but, considering that it was written in a back room of the Cavalry Barracks at Fort Laramie in 1961 under primitive conditions and more than 150 miles from good library facilities, I make no apologies for its content or its lack of sophistication. It was a pioneering effort in every sense and if it is helpful to others it will have served its purpose.

R.L.W.
National Trust for Historic Preservation
Washington, D.C.

INTRODUCTION

The bottles depicted herein were among artifacts recovered as a result of archaeological investigations at two great posts of the United States Army in the nineteenth-century trans-Mississippi West. Both Fort Laramie and Fort Union were established during the middle of the nineteenth century (Fort Laramie was purchased for an army garrison in 1849; Fort Union was founded in 1851). They were abandoned almost simultaneously, in 1890 and 1891 respectively. Both forts were founded in response to the westward drive of Americans in the first half of the century, and the role of both was to guard important routes of communication: roads, wires and mails. Fort Laramie was located beside the various overland trails of the all-important central route, the California, Oregon and Mormon roads. Fort Union was situated in the midst of the great Santa Fe trade route to the Southwest.

Although the mission of both posts was to guard the routes of westward movement, the nature of the journeys of those whom each guarded was quite distinct. Past Fort Laramie flowed thousands of men, women and children emigrating to the Far West. These were families with worldly goods in search of new homes and lives in a far land, people not fully aware that their actions were so expressive of the national will. But the caravans of canvas-covered wagons which struggled past Fort Union were vehicles of commercial expansion backed by men who consciously coveted the Southwest. Goods, not people, were the principal freight of the Santa Fe Trail, and the Southwest was added to the Union through economic association rather than by ties of blood. Despite these differences, Fort Laramie and Fort Union were both primary federal installations, for achieving the political goal of the nineteenth century — a continental nation.

The forts were located in the high arid plains, just under the mountains forming the continental divide, but little else in their physical nature was similar. There was only one Fort Laramie, although two privately owned fur trading posts of the same name had preceded the military installation. The army post was begun in 1849 with construction of a single building, and from that time grew in a random pattern. At its peak, in the 1870s, Fort Laramie resembled a small, untidy city. Its layout never experienced the hand of a planner. Its architecture displayed every conceivable variety and vicissitude of army style.

There were three Fort Unions too, but all were the work and property of the army. Each surpassed its predecessor in grandeur.

The first was a hastily built hodgepodge of unbarked logs. The second was a true fortification of earth. The third, on which construction began in 1863, was an unparalled example of army power and prestige of the time. By the 1870s Fort Union was a small city. Its buildings, from Officers' Quarters to Quartermaster Shops, were laid out in orderly clusters, displaying precise logic in the relationship of one building to another. Fort Union was the work of a master army planner who kept a tight grip on his compass and straight-edge. It sprang, full-grown, from his mind and changed little over the years.

Life at the two posts was probably very similar for garrison officers and their wives, enlisted men, laundresses and the children. Militarily, however, the histories were quite different. Fort Laramie was always a fighting post—a place where the gun-carrying enlisted man was typical. The energies of Fort Laramie involved mounting patrols, military escorts, scouts and expeditions for field service. Its troops were engaged in regular if not always intense confrontations with the Indian enemy, and they were killed to a man in the Grattan fight of 1854. Although not under siege, the post was constantly harassed by Indians throughout the period of the Civil War. Troops were sent from Fort Laramie to the Rosebud as well as countless lesser engagements, and John "Portugee" Phillips directed his horse toward Fort Laramie to aid Fort Phil Kearny. Even in the late 1870s, when the front line of Indian confrontation had receded far north of the post, Fort Laramie's primary mission was the support and replacement of troops actively engaged in the business of war.

Fort Union, on the other hand, was built to serve as a supply depot for the entire army of the Southwest. While troopers and soldiers from Fort Union participated in several important Southwestern campaigns (notably the Red River War of 1874 and the Battle of Soldier Spring in 1868), its overriding role, especially after construction of the vast third post, was to serve as an enormous regional supply depot for more remote posts engaged in most of the actual Indian fighting. Troopers at Fort Union were often outnumbered by civilian employees of the Quartermaster and Commissary Department.

Both forts were key establishments serving the cause of westward expansion. Both were abandoned when railroads replaced the wagon roads and settlement was well under way. Fort Union lay desolate from 1891 until 1956, becoming a vast acreage of standing walls and chimneys. Fort Laramie fell into civilian hands when the army marched away in 1890. Sold to settlers, some of its buildings were carried off to become parts of ranches and homesteads.

Bottles for all occasions, as well as a host of other artifacts, turned up in excavations for material culture at the Fort Union army post in New Mexico.

Others were occupied at their original sites by families and businesses. Parts of Fort Laramie survived almost intact, but most have vanished.

By the 1930s the sites of both posts were considered important indicators of the pioneering work which had helped to shape the nation. Fort Laramie and Fort Union were viewed as historically significant and were reclaimed by the United States and set aside as monuments to the past. Fort Laramie was designated a National Historic Site of the National Park Service in 1938, and Fort Union was established as a National Monument in 1956. The mission of the National Park Service at both was to interpret the role of the United States Army in the settlement of the trans-Mississippi West.

To fulfill this mission, the Park Service has attempted to retain and restore the buildings or fragments of remaining buildings. At Fort Union, these ruins have been stabilized and sprayed with a wind- and water-resistant compound. Those few buildings left intact at Fort Laramie are restored to their appearance during the heyday of the army, and some have been refurnished to help interpret the quality of life there. At both forts the larger story of their service is told in museum visitor centers.

Development of historic sites such as Fort Union and Fort Laramie depends almost wholly upon the fullest possible knowledge and understanding of their past. There is no shortage of information relating to their work, role, or physical characteristics: army records are voluminous, and civilian sources of information are numerous. But National Park Service researchers during the 1940s and early 1950s found a serious information gap on the quality of individual life at these places, and about the material details of life. Journals, diaries, and letters written by those who served at the posts contain material which fill portions of the gap, but no serious study has been made. It was evident that, while primary sources were indispensable, they did not contain enough data to permit proper interpretation of the sites. In short, information on the precise quality of life was limited and, as a consequence, the true human measure of service or sacrifice exacted by this phase of westward expansion was insufficiently known.

Archaeological work was then undertaken at both forts to shed light on this dim area, as well as to assist in documenting the larger physical and structural environment. A methodical excavation was planned and executed at Fort Union between 1956 and 1960. It included work at the site of the first rude post, and extensive digging at

View across Fort Laramie parade ground to Old Bedlam (restored). The enlisted men's quarters are to the left of Old Bedlam.

the last great fort. The work at the third post was undertaken for two reasons: to uncover and facilitate the stabilization of building walls, and to recover artifacts. All but nine of the ruins were excavated, and no important or representative feature was neglected. Particular attention was directed to the location of privies, and a number of these were fully excavated, yielding a remarkable quantity of excellent specimens.

Archaeological investigation at Fort Laramie has been less comprehensive and more problem- than project-oriented. Excavation has been undertaken on a sporadic basis since addition of the area to those of the National Park Service. Individual structures were excavated in the course of their restoration, a considerable amount of work has been directed to defining the limits of the first Fort Laramie, and the site of the second installation has been confirmed by archaeology. The site of the sutler's store has been excavated, as have the sites of several other trading posts in the vicinity of the fort. Fort Laramie has not, however, been the subject of a carefully planned, exhaustive archaeological investigation and, if we may judge by the wealth of artifacts that come to ground surface with every rain, a rich store of material and information is still recoverable.

The bottles presented in this work are the results of limited excavations and surface finds. While great numbers of other artifacts were found, the profusion and variety of bottles at both posts strongly impelled some study and report on them.

In addition to their importance as objects that can be used to date other historic sites, the bottles possess potential for contributing to broader areas of material culture studies, including questions of diet, recreation, medicine, and subtle social changes. In addition, they shed light on manufacturing processes and thus on the growth of the Industrial Revolution in this country. Furthermore, their very presence at these sites is eloquent testimony to the penetration of commercial systems of distribution and transportation. The primary concerns of this study, however, have been with identification and dating of the specimens.

Bottles of this study now form part of the collections at Fort Union and Fort Laramie. They have been catalogued in accordance with the system of classification reflected in the chapters of this work. While the abundance and excellence of the specimens are such that some may be placed as study collections in other institutions, notably the Smithsonian Institution, the collections of the National Park Service are representative and available to any interested scholar for further study.

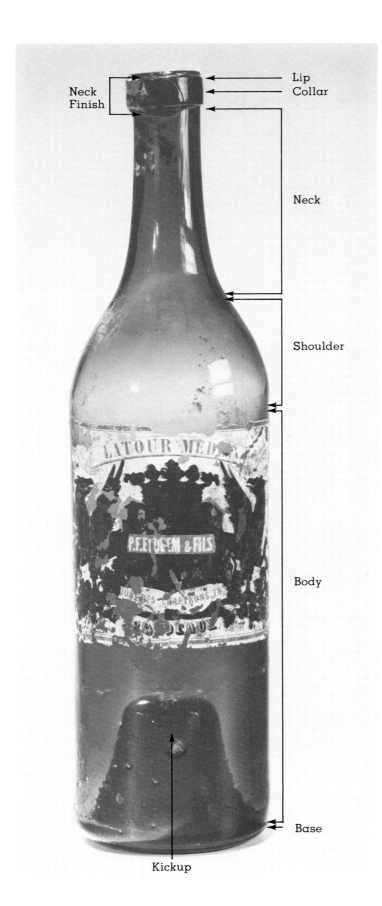

Neck
Finish

Lip
Collar

Neck

Shoulder

Body

Kickup

Base

Some of the terms used to describe bottle parts and material may not be familiar to all readers. The photographs accompanying the descriptions will, of course, help clarify the nomenclature. Still, the descriptions may be confusing to some degree.

Bottle experts are not consistent among themselves in their terminology of bottle shapes and finishes; hence, some of the terminology used in this book may not coincide with that elsewhere. The most complete, and most recent, glossary of bottle nomenclature can be found in the article by John R. White (see "Selected Readings"). Anyone interested in fully understanding the terms used should refer to this work. For a more immediate reference, on pages 110–11 are diagrams of bottle shapes and finishes taken from *Fort Bowie Material Culture* by Robert M. Herskovitz (No. 31 in the Anthropological Papers of the University of Arizona, 1978).

A short glossary, taken for the most part from White, is included here to aid those who do not wish to study the bottles in such detail.

Base: The bottom of the bottle, that is, the surface upon which it rests. Measurements of bases are taken where the diameter (or length and width) is greatest.
Body: The major portion of the bottle.
Collar: A band or belt applied as part of the neck finish and may be wide or narrow, rounded or flat. It is used to anchor the wire that holds the cork firmly in place, particularly on beer and wine bottles.
Finish: The upper terminus of the bottle's neck, designed to accommodate a tight-fitting stopper or closure to secure contents and usually added as a final step in the manufacture of a bottle. This finish may exist in a variety of shapes depending on the use for which the bottle was designed. Beer bottles, for example, commonly have a broad, rounded, or flat finish, often sloped, to which wire could be anchored to hold the cork in place. "Broad collared" means that this band, or belt, is conspicuously wide as contrasted to the finish of some other type of bottle.
Kick-up: A deep indentation of the base, common on wine bottles.
Lip: The edge of the bottle's mouth.
Mouth: The orifice or opening of the bottle.
Neck: The part of the bottle between the shoulder and the lip.
Panel: Rectangular insets on the sides of bottles with rectangular bodies.
Pontil mark: A circular basal scar commonly found on bottles made before the middle of the nineteenth century. Usually unsmoothed, the pontil mark is at the point where the blowing pipe was attached while the neck finish was being applied.
Shoulder: That part of the bottle between the neck and the body.
Stopper: A closure made to fit into the neck of the bottle to secure its contents.

SYMBOLS USED IN THE TEXT

" " All information, including punctuation, which appears between quotation marks refers to the historic information found on the bottles and labels.

( ) Information in roman type within parentheses serves to explain historic information—as a design or a picture of a horse—but the descriptive words do not themselves appear on the bottles or labels.

( ) Information in italics within parentheses is historic information that is known to have appeared on the bottles or labels but is not present on the specimen being described. That such historic information once appeared is known from referring to other specimens or other sources of historic data. Any question marks refer to information that is presumed or in question.

/ The slash signals the beginning of a new line.

. . . Ellipsis points indicate that there is a break in the bottle, or a tear, fading, smudge, or such in the label, through a word (or perhaps words). Historic data are insufficient to predict the complete word(s).

_____ A solid line is used where it is known that a complete word (or words) is missing, owing to a break in the specimen or a tear or such in the label.

In the years immediately after the Civil War a great swell of change transformed the industrial and social face of the United States. Included was the appearance of bottled beer on the frontier. A multitude of complex, intra-supportive developments occurred—among them the preference of Americans for a light lager of low alcoholic content, the development and application of pasteurization, and the drive of German-American brewers to expand their markets. All of these factors combined to produce a great beer boom in the West.

Lager beer, by its nature, was an unstable product until pasteurization made it possible to control bacteria. Prior to the 1870s, light beer was shipped only for very short distances. Its "keeping" qualities were so poor that within a few days after production it would sour and spoil. On the other hand, ales, stouts, or other beer-like beverages contained a higher alcoholic content which inhibited spoilage. Evidence of ales and stouts on the frontier are found at very early historic sites, but any fragile, lager beer in the West was almost certainly "home brew" until after 1873. In that year Adolphus Busch became the first brewer in this country to recognize the advantages of pasteurization and to introduce the process. National distribution of his pasteurized product began immediately. Other brewers soon followed suit, but Busch's early adoption of the process may explain the predominance of Anheuser-Busch bottles at Fort Union and Fort Laramie.

While the traditional, early beer bottle was ceramic, some glass containers were in use as early as the mid-eighteenth century. However, glass bottles were expensive and difficult to manufacture until industrial changes of the nineteenth century made volume production possible. Fortunately, this came at about the same time as the spread of pasteurization—a technique requiring use of inert, heatable, non-porous containers capable of accommodating an air-tight seal.

With these developments came yet another which has significance for the study of late-nineteenth century beer bottles, particularly those containers which still bear labels. Introduction of the pasteurization process almost immediately produced a subindustry of brewing. With the notable exception of Anheuser-Busch, most brewers of the period preferred to turn over the processes of pasteurization and bottling to a concessioner—a bottler—and to concentrate their own efforts on beer production. A single bottler sometimes handled the entire product of one brewery, adding his firm name to that of the brewer on the label. Bottles, therefore, often bear a closer relationship to the bottler than to the brewer, and it is not possible to identify a particular bottle style as that which typically contained a certain brand of beer.

The preference of brewers and bottlers for an amber glass container made in a style associated with "Export Beer" appears to have asserted itself very rapidly after the introduction of pasteurization and the use of glass bottles. Doubtless the industry saw in amber glass an additional protection from light and heat for their delicate product, but it is difficult to account for the popularity of the "Export"-style bottle, save to speculate that its shape was appealing because it was not customarily associated with other products. This was not true of the lager-style container which closely resembled a champagne bottle.

All developments discussed above are represented by the beer bottles found at Fort Union and Fort Laramie. We may assume that all contained a pasteurized lager beer, and date from after 1873. The practice of subcontracting bottling can be documented, and the trend toward the standard "Export"-style amber bottles may be traced. It remains only to account for the profusion of these bottles at both sites. The term profusion is an understatement when discussing incidence of beer bottles at the posts. Evidence indicates that the army of the late-nineteenth century on the western frontier drank a prodigious quantity of beer.

It is difficult to account for this popularity without resort to generalizations. Beer was cheap, and a soldier's pay small; it was thirst-quenching in an arid, dusty land; and it was essentially a new product, aggressively marketed. One fact, however, may be more significant than all of these generalizations. In 1881 a Presidential Order was issued prohibiting the sale of hard liquor by Post Traders to enlisted men on army posts, an order which confined soldiers' drinking to beer and wine. An outgrowth of the burgeoning temperance movement, and sad experience with heavy drinking in the army, the order merits at least the following query: would it have promulgated had not industrial processes developed a stable, low-alcohol, lager beer and made possible its widespread distribution in remote areas?

Whatever the reasons, it is evident that the nineteenth-century soldier on the frontier drank oceans of lager beer between 1873 and 1891. His enthusiasm for the beverage is evident in the numbers and large size of the bottles excavated. Hundreds of specimens were found minus their neck end, mute testimony to consumer impatience with the complex of wires, corks, and stoppers used to seal the product. In his eagerness to drink, the soldier often simply knocked off the bottle neck.

Among the multitude of specimens recovered at Fort Laramie and Fort Union, the bottles described here have primary interest as "type specimens." Because of their surviving labels, precise dating is possible.

1

2

3

1 Beer bottle. Lager style. Transparent, green glass. Molded with a wide-collar lip finish. Label: "ST. LOUIS LAGER BEER / TRADE (A & Eagle facsimile) MARK / Warranted to keep (in) (any) (climate) / Trade (MARK) / (GOLD) MEDAL." Height, 11 1/2 inches; base diameter, 3 1/8 inches. Capacity, about 24 ounces. Fort Union, 1879–83. No labels other than ST. LOUIS LAGER BEER, made by the Anheuser-Busch Brewing Association and dating between 1879 and 1883, were found on bottles of this style at either Fort Union or Fort Laramie.

2 Beer bottle. Export style. Transparent, green glass. Molded with a wide, convex lip finish. The label reads: "NEW MEXICO LAGER BEER / LAS VEGAS / BREWERY / & / BOTTLING / ASSOCIATION." Height, 11 9/16 inches; base diameter, 3 inches. Capacity, about 24 ounces. Fort Union, 1873–90. This bottle, found in the sutler's privy at Fort Union, indicates the availability of a local beer.

3 Beer bottle. Export style. Transparent, light-blue glass, bubbly texture. Molded with a wide, tapering-collar lip finish with a ring beneath. Inscription on the body: "C. CONRAD & CO'S / ORIGINAL / BUDWEISER / U.S. PATENT No. 6,376". Inscribed near the base: "D.O.C." The concave base is marked with the monogram, "C.C.Co. and BUDWEISER, U.S. PATENT 6,376." Height, 11 7/8 inches; base diameter, 3 inches. Capacity, about 24 ounces. Fort Union, 1877. Budweiser was first introduced in 1876 by Carl Conrad, in association with Adolphus Busch, at Conrad's celebrated downtown restaurant in St. Louis. In January, 1877, Conrad applied for a patent on the beer and marketed it in this light-blue bottle. Later that same year Conrad sold his interest in the beer to the E. Anheuser Company's Brewing Association, and that firm immediately began selling Budweiser under its own label. It is very unlikely that bottles bearing Conrad's name would have been manufactured after 1877.

4   Beer bottle. Transparent, pale blue glass with a broad, sloping-collar neck finish above a narrow, beveled ring. Molded body with the inscription: "C. CONRAD & CO.'S / ORIGINAL / BUDWEISER / U.S. PATENT Nº 6376." Centered in the base are the interlocking letters "C C & Co." Height, 11 11/16 inches; base diameter, 3 inches. Capacity, about 24 ounces. Fort Union, 1877–78.

5   Beer bottle. Transparent, pale blue glass with a broad cylindrical neck finish. Molded with a five-pointed star on the shoulder and an inscription on the body which reads: "Sᵀ L. B. B. Co." Around the perimeter of the base is the molded inscription: "O. K. H. T. G. S. (or backward Z)". Height, 11 1/4 inches; base diameter, 3 inches. Capacity, about 24 ounces. Fort Union, 1879–90.

4

5

6   Beer bottle. Export style. Transparent, amber glass. Molded with a cylindrical-collar lip finish with a ring beneath. Label: "Jos. Schlitz Brewing Co.'s / EXPORT / Milwaukee Lager Beer / TRADE MARK / Voechting, Shape & Co., / Sole Bottlers / Milwaukee, Wis. / H. GUGLER & SON, GEN-LITHOˢ. MIL-WAUKEE". Height, 11 9/16 inches; base diameter, 3 inches. Capacity, about 24 ounces. Fort Laramie, 1884. The Joseph Schlitz Brewing Company began using the label found on this specimen in 1877, when they established their bottling department as a separate enterprise operated by the Voechting, Shape Company. This bottle was found inside one of the plastered walls of an officer's quarters at Fort Laramie, having been put there during construction of that part of the building in 1884.

6

7   Beer bottle. Export style. Transparent, amber glass. Molded with a broad, sloping collar and with a surviving piece of wire indicating a wired-on cork stopper. Label: "Jos. Schlitz Brewing Cos. / EXPORT MILWAUKEE / WARRANTED TO KEEP / LAGER / TRADE MARK / BEER / GOOD LUCK / IN ANY CLIMATE / BREWED EXPRESSLY / FOR THE / American Bottling Co. / Chas. E. Meyer, Manager. Chicago, Ill. / THE MILWAUKEE LITHO & ENGR. CO." Centered in the base is the letter "H". Height, 11 11 / 16 inches; base diameter, 3 inches. Capacity, about 24 ounces. Fort Laramie, 1884. This specimen was found inside the same 1884 wall as bottle #6. Inasmuch as the Joseph Schlitz Company of Milwaukee delivered, beginning in 1877, all of its beer to the Voechting, Shape Company for pasteurizing and bottling, and considering the simultaneous deposit of the two bottles at Fort Laramie in 1884, it may be concluded that this specimen contained yet another imitative product, not made by *the* Joseph Schlitz Company of Milwaukee.

7

8

8 Beer bottle. Export style. Transparent, amber glass. Molded with a cylindrical-collared neck finish with a ring beneath. Label: "ST. LOUIS / TRADE / MARK / WARRANTED TO KEEP IN ANY CLIMATE / LAGER BEER / BOTTLING COMPANY." Medals read: "REPUBLIQUE / EXPOSITION UNIVERSALE INT . . . PARIS / AL / EXHIBITION / MDCCCLXXVI". Height, 11 7/16 inches; base diameter, 3 inches. Capacity, about 24 ounces. Fort Laramie, 1877–90. Several varieties of bottles, all bearing this St. Louis Lager Beer label, are common at Fort Laramie.

In May 1877, the E. Anheuser Co.'s Brewing Association obtained registration No. 4,623 for their A & Eagle trademark. The mark was reregistered under certificate No. 28,866 in 1896. The firm's St. Louis Lager Beer labels always carried these registrations, and their pre-1879 labels boasted of a medal won in 1876 in Philadelphia and another awarded in Paris in 1878. Details of the St. Louis Lager Beer labels on this specimen are significantly different from the Anheuser-Busch St. Louis Lager Beer label. It bears no company name, the A & Eagle trademark is missing, the medal in the center claims only an 1876 Philadelphia prize, and the patent number is missing. We may conclude that these bottles are not associated with Anheuser-Busch.

It is interesting that not a single label of this type was found at Fort Union, where Anheuser-Busch St. Louis Lager Beer labels occur in profusion. In this connection, it is important to remember that Fort Union was completely abandoned in 1891, although civilians continued to occupy Fort Laramie. It is possible that this bottle, or at least its product, dates after 1891. More important, however, is the wide variety of bottles found bearing this label. These range from typically shaped "Export" specimens to some of the 1877 blue bottles of C. Conrad for Budweiser. Although the evidence is complex, it seems to portray a marginal brewer marketing an imitative product in odds and ends of reused bottles, themselves which may conceivably date from as early as 1877 to some indeterminable time. They probably do not date later than the first decade of the 20th century, when a revolutionary new style of bottle closure dictated mass change in lip finish.

9

9 Beer bottle. Export style. Transparent, amber glass. Molded with a cylindrical-collar lip finish with a ring beneath. Obverse label reads: "ST. LOUIS LAGER BEER / TRADE (A & Eagle facsimile) MARK / NUMBER 4623 / ADOLPHUS BUSCH / ANHEUSER-BUSCH / BREWING / ASSOCIATION." Reverse label: "GOLD / MEDALS / PARIS 1878 / PHILADELPHIA 1876 / ON UNIVERSAL / NATIONAL DE / PHILADELPHIA / COMMISSION / MDCCCLXXVI / SEE THAT EVERY CORK / IS BRANDED ANHEUSERS / TRADE MARK REGISTERED 1877 / ADOLPHUS BUSCH." Height, 11 5/8 inches; base diameter, 3 1/8 inches. Capacity, about 24 ounces. Fort Union, 1879–83. If we may judge by the large number of bottles at Fort Union bearing this A-B label, St. Louis Lager Beer (a product of Anheuser-Busch) was either the most popular or, for a time, the only beer at the post. The label on this specimen dates the last filling between 1879 and 1883, the years during which this label was in use. In 1879 a label change was made following a change in the name of the company from the E. Anheuser Co.'s Brewing Association to the Anheuser-Busch Brewing Association. In 1883 the label was changed to display a medal awarded the beer in Amsterdam. In those days beer bottles were reused again and again, but labels were always removed in the washing process, and a new one applied each time the bottle was filled.

10 Beer bottle. Export style. Transparent, amber glass. Molded with a cylindrical-collar lip finish. Label: "Milwaukee / Bohemian / Export Beer / Brewed Expressly For Fine Trade And Made / Only From The Best Barley And Hops." Centered in the base is "20", circumscribed by: WIS. G. CO. / MILW." Height, 11 7/8 inches; base diameter, 3 inches. Capacity, about 24 ounces. Fort Laramie, 1884. This specimen, too, was found in the 1884 wall at Fort Laramie.

11 Beer Bottle. Transparent, pale blue glass with a broad, sloping-collar neck finish above a beveled ring. A molded body bears the inscription: "C. CONRAD & CO.'S / ORIGINAL / BUDWEISER / U.S. PATENT N⁰ 6376," and "D.O.C." Centered in the base are the interlocking letters "C C & Co." Height, 11 11/16 inches; base diameter, 3 inches. Capacity, about 24 ounces. Fort Laramie, 1877–78.

10   11

Two ancient malt beverages, ale and stout, were popular on the frontier long before the appearance of lager. Of higher alcoholic content than beer, these two beverages have a heady character that permitted relatively safe shipment over considerable distances before the time of pasteurization. This factor accounted for their appearance in New Mexico and other remote regions of the West in the 1850s, if not earlier.

Ale is a strong, fermented, aromatic malt beverage. It is darker, heavier, and more bitter than beer. Stout, a very dark ale, has a strong malt flavor and a sweet taste. A multitude of ale and stout bottles were recovered at Fort Union and Fort Laramie, many with remnants of paper labels or cork stoppers. Some of these bottles clearly predate beer bottles found at the same posts, and all indicate that Americans in the West brought with them a taste for these malt beverages.

The William Younger Company of Edinburgh, Scotland, now known as Scottish Brewers, Ltd., has been brewing ale since 1749. As early as 1805 the firm packaged its product in salt-glazed stoneware bottles. By the middle of the nineteenth century, Younger ale was enjoying great popularity in such metropolitan centers as St. Louis, New York, Chicago, and San Francisco, and some was shipped to the remote western frontier. The Younger bottles have been recovered from the first fort site at Fort

Union (1851–1861), and in large numbers from the third fort site (1863–1891). Some Younger bottles also turned up at Fort Laramie, many with original corks and foil seals in situ.

The William McEwan Company of Edinburgh also bottled some kind of beverage, probably ale, in similar salt-glazed stoneware.

Some ceramic bottles bear impressed stamps of their manufacturer, but most do not. These unlabeled, unstamped, salt-glazed bottles defy positive identification. Among the stamped bottles it has not been possible to associate any particular bottle marker with either the Younger or McEwan company or any other brewer.

Stout was bottled in dense-green glass bottles of two particular styles, and remnants of stout labels were found on both styles at Fort Union and Fort Laramie. Specific dates have not been assigned to the stout bottles. Some stout or porter may have been packaged in ceramic bottles, but no labels have been found as documentary evidence. Some bottle students assert that Scotch whiskey also was put up in clay bottles but again no labels have been found in situ to support the claim.

The following ale and stout bottles represent significant types.

12   Ale bottle. Salt-glazed, wheel-thrown stoneware. Cream body with a tan wash on a long neck. Gently sloping shoulder. Finished with a wide, sloping collar above a ring. Made by the Port Dundas Pottery, Glasgow, Scotland. Stamped within a circular impression at the base: "PORT DUNDAS POTTERY COY. / GLASGOW." The letter "W" is stamped immediately below. Height, 8 1/4 inches; base diameter, 3 inches. Capacity, about 15 ounces. Fort Union, 1863–90.

13   Ale bottle. Salt-glazed, wheel-thrown stoneware. Cream body with a tan wash on a short neck. Gently sloping shoulder. Finished with a narrow, sloping collar above a ring. Stamped at the base: "T / GROSVENOR / 3 / GLASGOW." Height, 8 3/8 inches; base diameter, 3 1/8 inches. Capacity, about 15 ounces. Fort Union, 1863–90.

14   Ale bottle. Salt-glazed, wheel-thrown stoneware. Cream body with a tan wash on a long neck. Gently sloping shoulder. Finished with an almost cylindrical collar and a ring. Stamped on the body near the base is "PORT DUNDAS / POTTERY COY / GLASGOW" with the Greek "Ω" immediately below. Height, 8 1/8 inches; base diameter, 3 inches. Capacity, about 15 ounces. Fort Union, 1863–90.

15   Ale bottle. Salt-glazed, wheel-thrown stoneware. Cream body with a tan wash on the neck. Gently sloping shoulder. Cylindrical collar, no ring. Stamped on the body near the base is "M KENNEDY / BARROWFIELD / 3 / POTTERY / GLASGOW". Height, 8 3/8 inches; base diameter, 3 1/16 inches. Capacity, about 15 ounces. Fort Union, 1863–90.

12

13

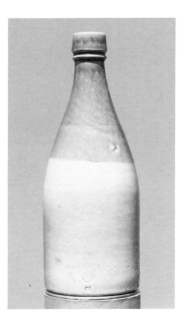

14

15

16

17

18

19

20

21

16 Ale bottle. Salt-glazed, wheel-thrown stoneware. Cream body with a tan wash on the neck. Slightly sloping shoulder. Ring-collar neck finish with a secondary ring beneath. The remnant of the paper label reads: "...ED ONLY BY WM. YOUNGER & Co. EDINBURGH / STRONG ALE / (picture of a building) / TRADE MARK / ...UNG.R & Co. / ...EY I... / _____ / ...CERY." Height, 8 1/4 inches; base diameter, 3 inches. Capacity, about 15 ounces. Fort Union, 1851–61.

17 Ale bottle. Salt-glazed, wheel-thrown stoneware. Cream body with a mottled tan wash on the neck, itself finished with a collar above a narrow ring. An impressed stamp near the base reads: "W". Height 8 1/2 inches; base diameter, 2 3/4 inches. Capacity, about 14 ounces. Fort Union, 1863–90.

18 Ale bottle. Salt-glazed, wheel-thrown stoneware. Cream body with a tan wash on the neck. Broad-collar neck finish above a narrow ring. An inscription on the body stamped near the base reads: "PORT DUNDAS / +GLASGOW+ / POTTERY COY." Height 8 1/8 inches; base diameter, 3 inches. Capacity, about 14 ounces. Fort Union, 1865–90.

19 Ale bottle. Salt-glazed, wheel-thrown stoneware. Cream body with a tan wash on the neck. Broad, rounded-collar neck finish above a narrow ring. Height, 7 5/8 inches; base diameter, 3 inches. Capacity, about 16 ounces. Fort Union, 1865–90.

20 Ale bottle. Salt-glazed, wheel-thrown stoneware. Cream body with a tan wash on the neck. Broad, cylindrical-collar neck finish above a narrow ring. Height, 7 5/8 inches; base diameter, 2 7/8 inches. Capacity, about 16 ounces. Fort Union, 1865–90.

21 Ale bottle. Salt-glazed, wheel-thrown stoneware. Cream body with a tan wash on the neck. Gently sloping shoulder. The neck is finished with a cylindrical collar above a narrow ring. Height, 8 3/8 inches; base diameter, 3 inches. Capacity, about 15 ounces. Fort Laramie, 1860–90.

22 Ale bottle. Salt-glazed, wheel-thrown stoneware. Cream body with a tan wash on the neck. Gently sloping shoulder. The neck is finished with a cylindrical collar. The remnant of the paper label begins: "YOUN...R & C᷎ / TRADE _____ / THIS LA... _____The remainder of the label, some 4 lines, is mostly unintelligible. Height 8 1/2 inches; base diameter, 2 7/8 inches. Capacity, about 15 ounces. Fort Laramie, 1850–60.

23 Ale bottle. Salt-glazed, wheel-thrown stoneware. Cream body with a tan wash on the neck. Gently sloping shoulder. The neck is finished with a cylindrical collar above a narrow ring. An illegible stamp appears near the base. Height, 8 7/16 inches; base diameter, 3 inches. Capacity, about 15 ounces. Fort Laramie, 1860–90.

22   **23**

24 Stout bottle. Transparent, dense-green glass with a broad-collar neck finish. Molded with "X I (raised dot) K" in the center of the base. Height, 9 1/2 inches; base diameter, 2 1/2 inches. Capacity, about 12 ounces. Fort Union, 1880–90.

25 Stout bottle. Molded. Transparent, green glass with a broad-collar neck finish above a narrow ring. Height, 9 1/4 inches; base diameter, 2 1/2 inches. Capacity, about 18 ounces. Fort Union, 1865–90.

24   **25**

26 Stout bottle. Dense-green glass. Molded with a gently sloping shoulder and narrow neck. Wide cylindrical collar. Label: "(E). & J. BURKE / (T)RAD(E) MARK / EJB (interlocking monogram) / ...TION (N)ONE GENUINE WITHOUT OUR PATE(NT) / _____ BEARING OUR TRADE MARK. / _____ John Burke (script) / D(U)BLIN / _____ FORE _____ STOUT."Red foil around the neck finish reads: "(BU)RKE / (TRADE) E & J B (monogram) MARK / DUBLIN" and on the opposite side "... wan (?) / BETT'S PATENT / TRADE (?) MARK." Base is marked with a raised dot in the center flanked by crudely executed letters "S" and "K". Height, 9 1/16 inches; base diameter, 2 5/8 inches. Capacity, about 14 ounces. Fort Laramie, 1870–75.

26

27

27 Stout bottle. Transparent, green glass with a broad, sloping-collar neck finish. Molded. The remnant of the label on the neck reads: "T. P. GRIFFIN & Co. / LONDON / TRADE MARK." Large raised dot in the center of the base. Height, 9 1/2 inches; base diameter, 2 5/8 inches. Capacity, about 14 ounces. Fort Laramie, 1870–80.

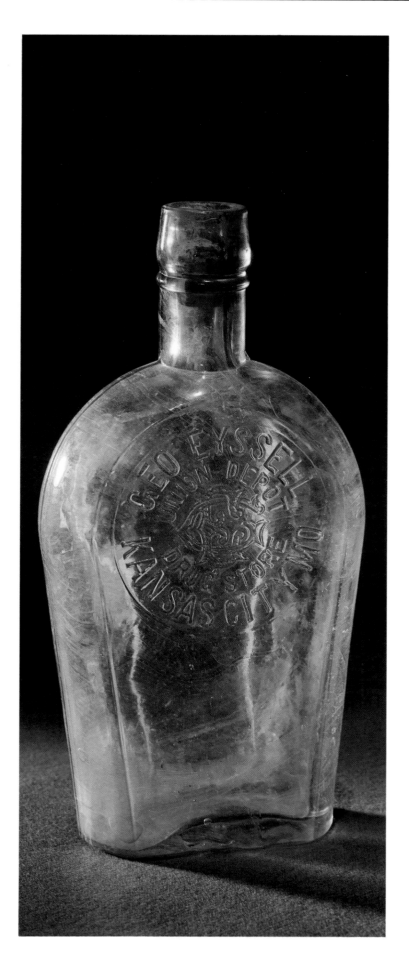

Whiskey made its appearance on the American frontier simultaneously with the first European men to set foot on any given piece of unexplored land. Comfort-bearing qualities of whiskey insured its presence, as did its commercial utility in the Indian trade. It was invulnerable to heat, cold, rough transport or time itself and if any beverage was typical of the drink of the frontier, surely whiskey must have been the one. In casks, kegs, and jugs, whiskey was there. It rarely arrived prepackaged in bottles, however. Most of the rye and bourbon whiskeys consumed on the frontier came out of the wooden casks in which they were shipped by anonymous distillers.

Brand names for whiskey first appeared after the Civil War in response to increased taxes and the resulting practice of storage in bond. Named whiskeys available in Colorado in 1883, and presumably available elsewhere in the West, had such colorful names as Tolu Rock & Rye, Brasher's Sour-Mash & Rye, Aurora Bourbon & Rye, Sunnyside All Rye, Oscar Pepper Sour-Mash & Rye, and McBrayers. Also on hand were more familiar names such as Hermitage & Old Crow. Prepackaged, name-branded whiskeys did not, however, become the standard medium of distribution until the passage of the Pure Food and Drug Act in 1906.

An occasional firm, such as the I. W. Harper Company, founded in 1872, packaged its product in colorless glass flasks as early as 1875. This practice appears to be an exception, however, and we may conclude that, for the most part, whiskey in the West was drained from bulk containers into a variety of bottles or other miscellaneous receptacles. Bartenders and sutlers doubtless kept their own supply of empty bottles which they filled for "package" sales and counter use, but they probably bore no labels or, if they did, the labels likely did not accurately reflect the nature of the contents. Dozens of unlabeled, straight-necked amber bottles that may have been used for bar sales were found at Fort Union and Fort Laramie, and many colorless flasks in several sizes were also found at the posts. Bottles of the amber type described appear in photographs of early saloons in the West.

At Fort Union bottles of the latter kind were found still bearing paper strip labels with "whiskey" written on them. Under the circumstances, it is not possible to associate specific specimens with a particular brand or type of whiskey. Neither can certain dates be assigned these bottles other than those which bracket the periods of use and deposit at Fort Union and Fort Laramie.

The appearance of gin and schnapps bottles at western army posts might be considered surprising. Actually, they only buttress the evidence of imported beverages documented by the Scottish ale and French wine bottles.

Gin and schnapps (Holland gin) are both redistilled beverages with common ancestry, but by the nineteenth century there were substantial differences in character and consumer. Holland gin, the parent beverage, was originally a medicinal made from barley mash which was distilled, rectified, and redistilled with juniper berry and other botanical flavorings. The result was a full-bodied malt beverage of high alcoholic content. The "gin" was brought to England by soldiers returning from the continent in 1792 and was altered there to become what is known as London Dry Gin, distilled from grain whiskey, rectified, flavored with juniper berries and other botanicals in a pot still, and redistilled. The result is a distinctively flavored drink of somewhat lesser proof than schnapps.

Traditionally, schnapps was favored by continental Europeans, while London gin came to be associated with the English. It is interesting to find bottles for both at the nineteenth-century posts in the American West—testimony to the heterogeneous peoples in army ranks.

28

29

28 Whiskey bottle. Excelsior oval, prescription lip. Transparent, colorless glass. Molded with the inscription on a rectangular body: "FINE WHISKIES / STEINWENDER & SELLNER / ST. LOUIS, MO." Height, 6 1/2 inches; base 2 3/4 × 1 1/2 inches. Capacity, about 11 ounces. Fort Union, 1871–90.

29 Whiskey bottle. Seal 322, plate-mold style. Transparent, colorless glass with a thickened, plain lip finish. Free-blown (?) with a crescent-shaped symbol below the shoulder. Height, 10 1/2 inches; base diameter, 2 1/4 inches. Capacity, about 18 ounces. Fort Union, 1860–90.

30

31

30 Whiskey bottle. Probably seal 322, plate-mold style. Transparent, colorless glass; finish type is unknown. The shoulder area is marked with a small crescent. Molded with an inscription on a cylindrical body: "PLANET / (man in crescent-shaped moon) / 75 SOUR MASH / FERO. WESTHEIMER & SONS." Molded in the center of the base are the joined letters "NB". Height, unknown; base diameter, 2 1/4 inches. Capacity, about 18 ounces. Fort Union 1875–90.

31 Whiskey bottle. Picnic flask. Transparent, colorless glass. Molded with a ring lip above a narrow ring. Height, 6 1/2 inches; base, 2 3/8 × 1 1/4 inches. Capacity, about 16 ounces. Fort Union, 1863–90.

32

33

32 Whiskey bottle. Picnic flask. Transparent, colorless glass. Molded with a broad-collar neck finish above a narrow ring. Height, 8 1/8 inches; base, 1 1/2 × 3 inches. Capacity, about 17 ounces. Fort Union, 1865–90.

33 Whiskey bottle. Picnic flask. Transparent, colorless glass. Molded with a ring lip above a narrow ring. Height, 8 inches; base, 2 7/8 × 2 inches. Capacity, about 16 ounces. Fort Union, 1865–90.

34 Whiskey bottle. Shoo-fly flask. Transparent, colorless glass with a broad, sloping-collar neck finish above a narrow rounded ring. Molded with a circular inscription on the upper part of the body: "GEO. EYSSELL / UNION DEPOT / (interlocking G & E monogram) / DRUG STORE / KANSAS CITY MO." Height, 7 3/4 inches; base, 3 × 1 3/4 inches. Capacity, about 15 ounces. Fort Union, 1875–90.

35 Whiskey bottle. Shoo-fly flask. Transparent, colorless glass. Molded with a broad, sloping-collar neck finish above the suggestion of a narrow ring. Height, 7 1/4 inches; base, 2 7/8 × 1 5/8 inches. Capacity, about 14 ounces. Fort Union, 1865–90.

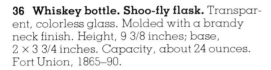

34

35

36 Whiskey bottle. Shoo-fly flask. Transparent, colorless glass. Molded with a brandy neck finish. Height, 9 3/8 inches; base, 2 × 3 3/4 inches. Capacity, about 24 ounces. Fort Union, 1865–90.

37 Whiskey bottle. Shoo-fly flask. Transparent, pale blue glass. Molded with a brandy neck finish. A molded inscription in the center of the base reads: "I. C Co" with the number "2" centered beneath and with a crudely executed "X" in upper right corner. Height, 6 1/4 inches; base, 2 5/8 × 1 1/4 inches. Capacity, about 8 ounces. Fort Union, 1865–90.

36

37

38 Whiskey bottle. Shoo-fly flask. Transparent, pale blue glass. Molded with a brandy neck finish. A molded inscription near the center of the base reads: "I G Co / B". Height, 7 1/8 inches; base, 3 × 1 1/2 inches. Capacity, about 13 ounces. Fort Union, 1863–90.

39 Whiskey(?) bottle. Transparent, colorless glass. Molded with a ring-lip neck finish above a narrow, beveled ring. Height, 5 1/4 inches; base, 1 1/4 × 1 3/4 inches. Capacity, about 8 ounces. Fort Union, 1863–90.

38

39

40

41

42

43

44

45

40 Whiskey bottle. Transparent, amber glass with a wide, sloping-collar lip above a narrow ring. Molded, cylindrical body with the inscription: "ONE QUART / YOU BET / JEWETT & ELY / OMAHA". Molded around the perimeter of the base: "WHITNEY GLASS WORKS GLASSBORO N J". Height, 12 1/4 inches; base diameter, 3 1/2 inches. Capacity, about 32 ounces. Fort Laramie, 1865–90.

41 Fluted flask, probably for whiskey. Transparent, molded, amber glass. The neck finish has a double ring lip. A ⊢)–(⊣ symbol appears in the base within a shallow, round depression. Height, 7 13/16 inches; base, 2 1/2 × 1 7/8 inches. Capacity, about 16 ounces. Fort Union, 1863–90.

42 Jug, probably for whiskey. Transparent, amber glass. Molded with a sloping neck finish and a single handle attached. Inscribed with a circular depression in the base are the letters "A C W Co". Height, 8 3/4 inches; base diameter, 2 7/8 inches. Capacity, about 27 ounces. Fort Union, 1863–90.

43 Whiskey flask, glass-stoppered. Transparent, molded, amber glass. The neck finish has a double ring lip above a narrow ring. Height, 7 5/8 inches; base, 3 3/8 × 1 1/2 inches. Capacity, about 16 ounces. Fort Laramie, 1885–90.

44 Schnapps bottle. Transparent, blue glass with a broad, sloping-collar neck finish. Molded with an inscription on a rectangular body: "CHARLES / LONDON / CORDIAL GIN". Height, 9 3/4 inches; base, 2 3/4 × 2 3/4 inches. Capacity, about 28 ounces. Fort Union, 1865–90.

45 Schnapps bottle. Transparent, amber-green glass with a broad, sloping-collar neck finish. Molded with an inscription on a rectangular body: "UDOLPHO WOLFE'S / SCHIEDAM / AROMATIC / SCHNAPPS". Height, 9 1/2 inches; base, 2 3/4 × 2 3/4 inches. Capacity, about 24 ounces. Fort Union, 1865–90.

46 Schnapps (?) bottle. Transparent, green glass. Molded with a broad, sloping-collar neck finish. Height, 9 1/2 inches; base, 3 × 3 inches. Capacity, about 30 ounces. Fort Union, 1860–90.

47 Plain schnapps bottle. Transparent, green glass. Molded with a broad, sloping-collar neck finish. Height, 7 7/8 inches; base, 2 1/4 × 2 1/4 inches. Capacity, about 14 ounces. Fort Union, 1865–75.

46   47

48 Gin bottle, square and tapered. Transparent, amber-green glass. Molded with a broad, sloping-collar neck finish. Recovered from the arsenal ruins, this specimen may be associated with the immediately adjacent site of the first Fort Union. A crude diamond is outlined in the center of the base. Height, 9 3/8 inches; base, 2 3/8 inches square. Capacity, about 27 ounces. Fort Union, 1851–78.

49 Liquor bottle. Transparent, amber glass. Molded with a broad, sloping-collar neck finish above a ring and with continuous threads inside. The molded inscription around the perimeter of the oval base reads: "WHITNEY / GLASS WORKS." Height, 7 7/8 inches; base, 2 × 3 1/8 inches. Capacity, about 18 ounces. Fort Union, 1865–90.

48   49

Perhaps the most "civilized" aspect of the frontier at army posts was the sutler's wine list, and Fort Union and Fort Laramie yielded many wine bottles which contribute to the evidence. The records of Fort Laramie's post trader reveal that he offered American, French, and Spanish wines to his clientele in the 1880s. His cellar contained clarets, sherries, and sweet dessert wines, as well as such enviable delicacies as "Mumms" champagne and a Bordeaux from one of the premiers chateaux in all of France. Indeed, there were some times and places in the settlement of the West when the traditional life of hardship was very comfortable ornamented!

If the number of wine bottles found at the two forts is any indication, champagne was an army favorite. Its typically heavy green bottle with a depression or kick-up in the base predominates. The character of champagne requires this type of bottle with heavy walls and gentle lines designed to withstand pressures generated by refermentation. The nineteenth-century, handmade, blown-molded champagne bottle is nearly identical to a modern one, except for the hand-finished lip.

Other wines that have been bottled and corked since the late seventeenth century were not packaged in bottles distinctive of original contents. Rather, the bottles that appear to have contained wines, brandies, or cordials display a wide variety of shapes, designs, and colors, and it is not possible to date or trace any of them with certainty.

Wines were always available for sale to enlisted men, but they preferred beer or, until 1881, whiskey. Doubtless most wine was consumed by the officers of the posts. The records of the post trader at Fort Laramie show a distinct increase in wine sales around Thanksgiving and Christmas. This may indicate an increased seasonal interest in wine on the part of enlisted men or, perhaps, an increase in consumption on the part of all.

50 Wine bottle. Transparent, amber glass with a wine neck finish. Molded. Evenly spaced around the perimeter of the base are eight large dots slightly raised. Height, 13 3/8 inches; base diameter, 2 7/8 inches. Capacity, about 24 ounces. Fort Union, 1885–90.

51 Wine bottle. Transparent, amber glass. Molded with a wine neck finish. Height, 6 3/8 inches; base, 1 3/4 × 2 inches. Capacity, about 15 ounces. Fort Union, 1865–90.

50   51

52 Wine bottle. Salt-glazed, wheel-thrown, brown stoneware, with a wine neck finish. Impressed on the shoulder is "EX-OPTIMO / 1875." An additional small, but illegible, impressed stamp appears near the edge of the circular base. Height, 8 1/2 inches; base diameter, 3 1/8 inches. Capacity, unknown. Fort Union, 1875.

53 Wine(?) bottle. Transparent, blue glass. Molded with a thickened, plain-lip neck finish. Height, 10 3/4 inches; base diameter, 2 1/2 inches. Capacity, about 16 ounces. Fort Union, 1860–80.

52   53

54

55

54 Wine bottle. Transparent, colorless glass. Molded with a plain-lip neck finish. The base has a kick-up. Height, 11 5/8 inches; base diameter, 2 5/8 inches. Capacity, about 24 ounces. Fort Laramie, 1870–90.

55 French wine bottle. Transparent, light-green glass with a deep kick-up in the base. Probably free-blown. The remnant of the paper label reads: "LATOUR MEDOC / P.F. ...UEM & FILS / QUA(I?) (D?)ES CHARTRONS, 78. / BORDEAUX." Height, 11 7/8 inches; base, about 3 inches. Capacity, about 26 ounces. Fort Union, 1863–90.

56

57

56 Brandy or wine bottle. Transparent, amber glass. Molded with a broad, sloping-collar neck finish above a narrow ring. The legend "AMERICAN VINTAGE C°" is inscribed around the shoulder. Height, 11 5/8 inches; base, 2 15/16 inches. Capacity, about 22 ounces. Fort Union, 1863–90.

57 Brandy bottle. Transparent, deep-amber glass. Molded with a broad, sloping-collar neck finish above a narrow ring. A molded inscription on the body reads: "W^M CARL & C / SANTA FEE / N M". Height, 8 15/16 inches; base, 3 3/4 inches. Capacity, about 27 ounces. Fort Union, 1863–90.

58

59

58 Brandy (?) bottle. Transparent, amber glass. Molded with a broad, sloping-collar neck finish above a narrow ring. Height, 11 7/8 inches; base diameter, 3 3/8 inches. Capacity, about 26 ounces. Fort Laramie, 1880–90.

59 Cognac bottle. Transparent, amber glass. Molded with a broad-collar neck finish above a narrow ring. The remnant of the paper label indicates the original contents to have been "OLD / COGNAC BRANDY." Height, 10 3/4 inches; base diameter, 2 3/4 inches. Capacity, about 26 ounces. Fort Union, 1865–90.

Bitters containers are among the most imaginatively shaped and interesting of all old bottles. Although bitters makers appear to have favored a square bottle of amber glass, they often distributed their product in clear or green glass bottles shaped to distinguish their brand. These containers represent some of the earliest efforts of manufacturers to attract buyers in a highly competitive field through packaging, as well as product appeal.

Developed originally in the sixteenth century as a medicinal, bitters was a beverage extracted from a variety of substances (gentian root, hop flowers, quinine, and bitter orange peel, among others) to which an aromatic flavoring (juniper, cinnamon, caraway, nutmeg, etc.), alcohol, and sometimes sugar were added. The alcoholic content was sometimes as much as 40 percent, and the drink today is considered to have no medicinal value.

In the nineteenth century, however, manufacturers claimed all kinds of restorative and curative powers for their product. Bitters would, its makers said, cure dyspepsia, constipation, diarrhea, cholera, liver complaint, malaria, nervous headache, and overindulgence. It would strengthen the weak, rest the fatigued, comfort the traveler, and make a dull mind witty. It was recommended for children and adults, and it is easy to understand the enormous popularity of the beverage after 1850 given its proclaimed hygienic virtues and alcoholic content.

In the nineteenth century, bitters could be consumed without censure or guilt by women or others finding themselves in an environment influenced by the temperance movement. Doubtless there were guileless souls who took it regularly, sincerely believing in its medicinal value, as well as confirmed drinkers who cared not at all about its health benefits as long as its alcoholic content held up. Acceptance of the drink, as evidenced by its large containers so highly competitive for attention, must repose in the fact that it gave pleasure behind the mask of need.

The following bitters bottles, recovered at Fort Union and Fort Laramie, testify to the far-flung popularity of the beverage.

60 Bitters bottle. Transparent, amber glass with a broad, sloping-collar neck finish. Molded with an inscription on the body: "S.T. DRAKE / 1860 / PLANTATION / X / BITTERS / PATENTED / 1862." Height, 10 1/16 inches; base diameter, 2 7/8 inches. Capacity, about 30 ounces. This fine specimen duplicates fragmentary bottles from both Forts Union and Laramie but was not recovered from either site. 1862–85.

61 Bitters bottle. Paneled schnapps style. Transparent, amber glass with a broad, sloping-collar neck finish. Molded with an inscription inside a panel on the rectangular body: "I & L M HELLMAN," and inside the panel on the opposite side: "SᵀLOUIS. Mᵒ." This specimen may possibly have contained whiskey. Height, 8 5/8 inches; base, 2 3/4 × 2 3/4 inches. Capacity, about 24 ounces. Fort Union, 1863–90.

60   61

62 Bitters bottle. Paneled and columned schnapps style. Transparent, amber glass. Molded with an inscription on a rectangular body: "GARNHART & KELLY / SᵀLOUIS Mᵒ." This specimen may possibly have contained whiskey. Height, unknown; base, 2 3/4 × 2 3/4 inches. Capacity, about 20 ounces. Fort Union, 1863–65.

63 Bitters bottle. Transparent, colorless glass. The neck is finished with a thickened, plain lip. Molded, with an inscription near the base of the rectangular body: "ILER & Co. / OMAHA NEB." Near the base of the shoulder is inscribed: "KENNEDYS / EAST INDIA / BITTERS". A fragment recovered near Fort Laramie is apparently from a bottle identical to this specimen which contained Kennedy's East India Bitters. Height, 9 inches; base, 2 7/8 × 2 7/8 inches. Capacity, about 30 ounces. Fort Union, 1872–90.

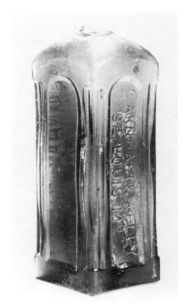

62   63

64

65

64 Bitters bottle. Paneled schnapps style.
Transparent , amber glass with a broad, sloping-collar neck finish. Molded with an inscription on the rectangular body: "JA.ˢ A. JACKSON & CO / PROPRIETORS / HOME BITTERS / SAINT LOUIS M.ᵒ". Height, 9 1/8 inches; base, 2 3/4× 2 3/4 inches. Capacity, about 20 ounces. Fort Union, 1866–76.

65 Bitters bottle. Paneled schnapps style.
Transparent, amber glass with a broad, sloping-collar neck finish. Molded with an inscription on the rectangular body: "D.ᴿ J HOSTETTER'S / STOMACH BITTERS". Labels found on Hostetter bottles at Fort Union are dark blue with black lettering. Height, 8 3/4 inches; base, 2 3/4 inches × 2 3/4 inches. Capacity, about 22 ounces. Fort Union, 1865–85.

66

67

66 Bitters bottle. Double-ball-neck style.
Transparent, amber-green glass with a broad, sloping-collar neck finish. Molded with an inscription on the body: "C. LEDIARD / ST. LOUIS." Other bottles of this type found at Fort Union were amber, and inscribed "C. FEDERAL / NEW YORK." Height, 11 inches; diameter of the hexagonal base, 3 1/8 inches. Capacity, about 25 ounces. Fort Union, 1866–71.

67 Bitters bottle. Square, tapered gin style.
Transparent, amber glass with a broad, sloping-collar neck finish above a narrow, beveled ring. Molded with an inscription on a rectangular body: "C. LEDIARD / Sᵀ LOUIS." A circular basal depression is marked with a raised cross which separates the area into quadrants. Height, 10 inches; base diameter, 2 1/4 inches. Capacity, about 20 ounces. Fort Union, 1866–71.

68

69

68 Bitters bottle. Paneled, schnapps style.
Transparent, amber glass with a broad, sloping-collar neck finish. Molded with an inscription on the body: "PARKERS / CELEBRATED / (monogram) / STOMACH / BITTERS". A base marking reads: "I. G. Co." Height, 9 1/4 inches; base, 2 5/8 × 2 5/8 inches. Capacity, about 24 ounces. Fort Union, 1865–75.

69 Bitters bottle. Transparent, amber glass. Broad, rounded-collar neck finish above a beveled ring. Molded to represent a pineapple, this bottle may originally have contained pineapple bitters, although the same bottle was often used for whiskey. Attributed to the Whitney Glass Company of Glassboro, New Jersey. Height, 9 1/8 inches; base diameter, 3 3/4 inches. Capacity, about 21 ounces. Fort Union, 1865–75.

70 Bitters bottle. Paneled, schnapps style.
Transparent, amber glass with a broad, sloping-collar neck finish. Molded with an inscription on a rectangular body: "SCHWAB PIETERS & CO / RED JACKET / BITTERS". The base marking is that of the William McCully Company of Pittsburgh, Pa. Height, 9 5/8 inches; base, 2 3/4 × 2 3/4 inches. Capacity, about 24 ounces. Fort Union, 1865–75.

71 Bitters bottle. Transparent, amber-glass whiskey flask. Thickened, plain-lip neck finish with a narrow, beveled fillet below. On one side of the molded body is depicted a phoenix with the word "RESURGAM" below. On the reverse side is an anchor and the inscription "BALTIMORE GLASS WORKS." Height, 7 5/8 inches; base, 3 1/8 × 2 inches. Capacity, about 16 ounces. Fort Union, 1850–55.

 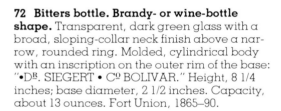

70   71

72 Bitters bottle. Brandy- or wine-bottle shape. Transparent, dark green glass with a broad, sloping-collar neck finish above a narrow, rounded ring. Molded, cylindrical body with an inscription on the outer rim of the base: "•D͞R. SIEGERT • C͞O BOLIVAR." Height, 8 1/4 inches; base diameter, 2 1/2 inches. Capacity, about 13 ounces. Fort Union, 1865–90.

73 Bitters bottle. Paneled schnapps style.
Transparent, amber glass with a broad, sloping-collar neck finish. Molded with an inscription on the body: "WEST INDIA / STOMACH BITTERS / ST. LOUIS MO". The base is inscribed with "WIMC͞O". Height, 8 1/2 inches; base, 2 3/4 × 2 3/4 inches. Capacity, about 23 ounces. Fort Union, 1865–75.

72   73

74 Bitters(?) bottle. Paneled. Transparent, amber glass. Molded with a broad, sloping-collar neck finish. Height, 10 1/4 inches; base, 3 5/8 × 2 1/8 inches. Capacity, about 24 ounces. Fort Union, 1865–85.

75 Bitters bottle. Transparent, amber glass with an unknown neck finish. Two body surfaces are vertically reeded; the third is paneled. Molded with an inscription near the shoulder: "O K / PLANTATION / 1840." Height, unknown; base, 3 × 3 × 3 inches. Capacity, unknown. Fort Union, 1865-75.

74   75

76

77

76 Bitters bottle. Transparent, green glass with an unknown neck finish. Molded with an inscription around the shoulder: "D^R J G B SIEGERT & HIJOS." This is repeated around the perimeter of the base. Height, unknown; base diameter, 2 1/2 inches. Capacity, about 8 ounces. Fort Union, 1870–90.

77 Bitters bottle. Brandy or wine bottle shape. Transparent, green glass with a broad, sloping-collar neck finish above a narrow ring. Molded with an inscription around the shoulder: "DR J G B SIEGERT & HIJOS." The same inscription occurs on the base of the bottle. Height, 8 3/8 inches; base diameter, 2 7/16 inches. Capacity, about 11 ounces. Fort Laramie, 1865–90.

The manufacture, bottling, and distribution of soda water has its roots in the popularity of natural, sparkling mineral waters, long considered medicinally valuable and safe even in the centuries before sanitary controls were placed on public water systems. Artificially carbonated or mineralized water was not developed, however, until late in the eighteenth century, and it was introduced in this country early in the nineteenth. The idea of flavoring this water with fruit juices, spices, extracts, aromatic roots, and sugar syrups followed rapidly. In general then, soda-water bottles could be expected to turn up at western army posts in very early periods.

Carbonation of such beverages prevented spoilage and permitted their shipment to distant places, even before refrigeration or pasteurization. The same factor dictated typical container shape. Heavy walls, like those of champagne bottles, were required to withstand the pressure of the contents; round bottoms were intended to insure that bottles lay on their sides, a position in which corks would not dry out, shrink, or be forced out by the pressurized contents; and thick collars were needed to withstand outward thrust of the wired-on cork. This basic bottle shape endured until patented wire and rubber stoppers eliminated the need for the round bottom.

In documenting the technical development of patented stoppers, soda bottles with round (and others with flat) bottoms were found at the forts. A few stoppers were found (predominately the Hutchinson stopper), and in a few cases at Fort Union they were still inserted in the bottles. Although stoppers were found at Fort Laramie, none appeared in association with a bottle.

Soda-water beverages, whether plain or flavored, doubtless owed much of their popularity at western army posts to their traditional virtues of purity and therapy. Water supplies at army installations were notoriously poor, and even modern medicine recognizes the usefulness of these liquids for indigestion and nausea and for maintaining body fluids during illness.

78 Soda-water bottle. Transparent, pale blue glass. Broad, rounded-collar neck finish. Molded with an inscription on the body, within a circle: "SCHERER & WIEGAND / LAS VEGAS / NM". Part of a Hutchinson stopper in situ. Height, 6 3/8 inches; base diameter, 2 1/2 inches. Capacity, about 10 ounces. Fort Union, 1870–90.

79 Soda-water bottle, ginger ale. Light-green glass. Round-bottomed with a broad-collar neck finish. Molded with an inscription on a cylindrical body: "ROSS'S / BELFAST". Height, 9 3/8 inches; base diameter, 2 3/8 inches. Capacity, about 12 ounces. Fort Union, 1875–90.

80 Soda-water bottle, ginger ale. Transparent, green glass. Round-bottomed with a broad-collar neck finish. Molded with an inscription on the body: "ROSS'S / BELFAST". In 1877 Belfast was advertised in Washington, D.C. at $2.00 per dozen bottles. Height, 9 3/8 inches; base diameter, 2 3/8 inches. Capacity, about 12 ounces. Fort Union, 1875–90.

81 Soda- or mineral-water bottle. Hutchinson's patent style designed for use with the Hutchinson patent stopper. Transparent, light-blue glass with a broad, rounded-collar neck finish. Molded with an inscription on a cylindrical body: "C WIEGAND / LAS VEGAS / NM". Height, 6 3/4 inches; base diameter, 2 1/2 inches. Capacity, about 8 ounces. Fort Union, 1880–90.

78

79

80

81

82

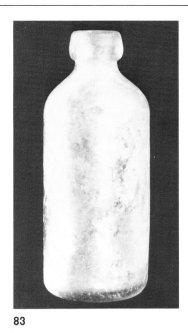

83

84

85

86

87

82 Soda- or mineral-water bottle. Transparent, light-green glass. Two lateral depressions immediately under the broad, rounded-collar neck finish. These depressions were provided to accommodate a wire clamp which, in turn, held some sort of stopper in place, probably the "Lightning." Molded with an inscription on a cylindrical body: "C. A. SCHEIDEMANTEL / DENVER COL". Height, 7 7/8 inches; base diameter, 2 3/8 inches. Capacity, about 10 ounces. Fort Union, 1875–85.

83 Soda- or mineral-water bottle. Transparent, pale blue glass. Molded with a broad, rounded-collar neck finish. Height, 6 5/8 inches; base diameter, 2 3/8 inches. Capacity, about 11 ounces. Fort Union, 1865–90.

84 Soda-water bottle. Light-blue glass. Nearly pointed round base, with a broad, sloping, rounded-collar neck finish. This molded specimen contained English Club Soda bottled by Chesterman and Barrow Company. Height, 8 13/16 inches; maximum base diameter, 2 7/8 inches. Capacity, about 11 ounces. Fort Laramie, 1883.

85 Soda-water bottle. Transparent, blue glass. Broad, sloping-collar neck finish. Molded with an inscription on the body: "JONES SIBLEY & Co / S^T LOUIS Mo". Mold lines divide the base of this specimen into five pie-shaped zones. Height, 8 7/8 inches; base diameter, 2 3/8 inches. Capacity, about 11 ounces. Fort Laramie, 1870–90.

86 Soda-water bottle, ginger ale. Light-blue glass. Round-bottomed, with a broad, rounded-collar neck finish. Molded with an inscription on a cylindrical body: "SEE THAT EACH CORK IS BRANDED / CANTRELL & COCHRANE." Across spherical base: "DUBLIN / & / BELFAST." Height, 9 3/8 inches; base diameter, 2 3/8 inches. Capacity, about 11 ounces. Fort Laramie, 1875–85.

87 Soda-water bottle, ginger ale. Light-blue glass. Round-bottomed, with a broad-collar neck finish. Molded with an inscription on a cylindrical body: "CANTRELL / & / COCHRANE / BELFAST / & / DUBLIN." Height, 9 3/16 inches; base diameter, 2 3/8 inches. Capacity, about 11 ounces. Fort Laramie, 1875–85.

88 Soda-water bottle, ginger ale. Light-blue glass. Round-bottomed, with a broad, rounded-collar neck finish. Molded with an inscription on the base: "C. & B. / LE MARS / IA". Used by the Chesterman and Barrow Company between 1882 and 1885. Height, 9 11/16 inches; base diameter, 2 3/8 inches. Capacity, about 11 ounces. Fort Laramie, 1882–85.

89 Seltzer-water jug. Salt-glazed, wheel-thrown stoneware with a ringed neck and a ring-lip neck finish. Reddish orange color. Stamped on the body is: "B / NUM 37 / • SEKTERS • / NASSAU (within a circle) / (crowned eagle in the center of a circular stamp)". Height, 11 5/8 inches; base diameter, 3 7/16 inches. Capacity, about 40 ounces. Fort Laramie, 1860–90.

88   89

When army people received an assignment to a western post in the nineteenth century, they could expect to encounter illness and hazard to a greater degree than in the East. This, together with the primitive stage of development in medical science, may account for many bottles at Fort Laramie and Fort Union which once contained potions intended to cure all manner of disease and to remedy a variety of physical ailments.

Digestive problems appear to have outnumbered all other physical discomforts in the West, owing possibly to the chemistry of western water, the poor sanitary conditions at army posts, and to dietary restrictions resulting from policies of the Commissary Department and the slowness or absence of transport.

Among preparations designed to support good health, essence of ginger seems to have been very effective and popular. Numerous bottles once containing ginger were found at both forts in sufficient quantity to suggest that it was a favored remedy.

For medicinal purposes, ginger was ground and added to a beverage—brandy in many instances. While the final product contained alcohol, the small size of the bottles in which it was marketed indicates that the resulting concoction was used primarily as medicine and not as a beverage of pleasure such as bitters. Ginger was reputed to cure cholera, cholera morbus, cramps and pains, diarrhea and dysentery, dyspepsia, flatulence, want of tone and activity in the stomach and bowels, and to ameliorate health problems brought on by a change in climate, water, and food. In fact, ginger is a carminative, stimulant, rubefacient and counterirritant.

Ginger bottles found at Forts Union and Laramie are remarkably similar in design and size. Their prime interest derives from the impressed legends on the bottles.

The following advertisement appeared in one issue of the *Center-Union Agriculturist* in 1878:

SANFORD'S JAMAICA GINGER

The only combination of the true Jamaica Ginger with choice aromatic and French brandy for cholera, cholera morbus, cramps and pains, diarrhoea and dysentery, dyspepsia, flatulency, want of tone and activity in the stomach and bowels, and avoiding the dangers of change of water, food and climate. Ask for SANFORD'S JAMAICA GINGER.

90 Ginger bottle. Drug oval, patent lip.
Transparent, light-green glass with a thickened, plain-lip neck finish. Molded with an inscription on the rectangular body: "F. BROWN'S / ESS OF / JAMAICA GINGER / PHILAD^A". Height, 5 1/2 inches; base, 2 1/4 × 1 1/4 inches. Capacity, about 4 ounces. Fort Union, 1865–90.

91 Ginger bottle. Plain, oval, patent lip.
Transparent, blue glass with a thickened, plain-lip neck finish. Molded with an inscription on the body: "N. K. BROWN'S / AROMATIC ESSENCE / JAMAICA GINGER / BURLINGTON, VT." Height, 6 inches; base, 2 1/4 × 1 1/4 inches. Capacity, about 6 ounces. Fort Union, 1865–90.

90   91

92 Ginger bottle. Philadelphia oval. Transparent, colorless glass with a thickened, plain-lip neck finish. Molded with an inscription on the body: "GILLETT'S / ESS JAMAICA / GINGER / (monogram and seal) / F. W. GILLETT / CHICAGO." Height, 5 3/8 inches; base, 2 1/4 × 1 1/4 inches. Capacity, about 6 ounces. Fort Union, 1865–90.

93 Ginger bottle. Plain oval, deep lip.
Transparent, green glass with a broad, rounded-collar neck finish. Molded with an inscription on the body: "MELLIER'S / ESS. OF / JAMAICA GINGER / S^T LOUIS." Height, 5 3/4 inches; base, 2 1/4 × 1 1/4 inches. Capacity, about 5 ounces. Fort Union, 1880–90.

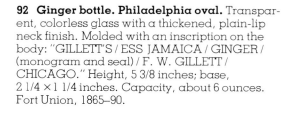

92   93

94

95

96

97

94 Ginger bottle. Drug oval, deep lip. Transparent, light-blue glass with a broad, sloping, and rounded-collar neck finish. Molded with an inscription on the body: "MEYER'S / ESS OF / JAMAICA GINGER / ST. LOUIS." Height, 5 5/8 inches; base, 2 3/8 ×1 3/8 inches. Capacity, about 6 ounces. Fort Union, 1865–90.

95 Ginger bottle. Transparent, pale blue glass with broad, sloping-collar neck finish. A remnant of the paper label reads: "BROWN'S / HIGHLY / CONCENTRATED / ESSENCE / JAMAICA / GINGER". Height, 5 1/4 inches; base, 1 1/4 ×2 1/8 inches. Capacity, about 6 ounces. Fort Union, 1865–1890.

96 Ginger bottle. Tall ginger oval. Transparent, pale blue glass with a broad, sloping-collar neck finish. Molded with an inscription on the body: "F. BROWN'S / ESS OF / JAMAICA GINGER / PHILAD^A". Height, 5 1/2 inches; base, 1 1/4 ×2 1/4 inches. Capacity, about 6 ounces. Fort Union, 1865–80.

97 Ginger bottle. Tall ginger oval. Transparent, pale blue glass with a double-ring neck finish. Molded with an inscription on the body: "MELLIER'S / ESS. OF / JAMAICA GINGER / ST. LOUIS". Height, 5 3/4 inches; base, 1 1/4 ×2 1/4 inches. Capacity, about 5 ounces. Fort Union, 1863–90.

Mineral waters have been known for their therapeutic qualities for centuries and have been used to treat various human ailments, primarily of the digestive system. Effervescent waters containing carbon dioxide aid in digestion to the extent that man ultimately sought to make them artificially. Other waters, particularly those containing sulphur or magnesia salts in solution, have proven extremely useful for the treatment of cathartic problems.

Traditionally, people desiring benefits of mineral waters made pilgrimages to the springs that were their sources. In the nineteenth century, firms began to bottle such natural waters and made them available to individuals at considerable distances from the source. Mineral-water bottles found at Fort Laramie and Fort Union testify to the breadth of their distribution by the latter half of the nineteenth century. It is worth noting, however, that few such bottles were found at the forts. The two bottles which represent this group contained mineral waters useful for their cathartic properties, while numerous bottles were found which contained remedies for dysentery or diarrhea. This interesting proportion may be explained by the highly alkaline nature of many western waters. The human condition is determined in part by its environment, and this ratio of bottles may document that simple fact.

The following advertisement appeared in one issue of *The Daily Inter Ocean*, Chicago, Illinois, in 1885.

HUNYADI JANOS

Hunyadi Janos the best and cheapest natural aperient water...the most certain and comfortable cathartic in cases of sluggish liver or piles. Ordinary dose, a wine-glassful before breakfast. Of all druggists and mineral water dealers. None genuine but with the blue label.

98 Mineral-water bottle. Transparent, emerald green glass with a broad, sloping-collar neck finish above a narrow, beveled ring. A molded inscription reads: "CONGRESS / WATER" on one side of the cylindrical body, and "HOTCHKISSON'S / C (very large) / NEW YORK / SARATOGA N. Y." framed by "CONGRESS & EMPIRE SPRING CO" on the other side. A cross is molded in the center of a concave base. Height, 7 3/4 inches; base diameter, 3 inches. Capacity, about 20 ounces. Fort Union, 1866–90.

99 Mineral-water bottle. Transparent, green glass with a broad, rounded neck finish. The remnant of the paper label reads: "APOL... NA... / APOLLINARIS _____ / ...EGENT." In a box to the left side: "This Bottle / should be / laid on its / side in a / co(ol?) (pla?)ce", and across the bottom is "S...LE A...FOR THE / F (or E) R... PLACE." This product was referred to as "The queen of table waters" in *The Daily Inter Ocean* in 1885. Height, 9 1/4 inches; base diameter, 2 5/8 inches. Capacity, about 16 ounces. Fort Union, 1875–90.

98

99

The nineteenth century was the heyday for proprietary medicines, and nowhere was this more evident than in the American West. A combination of forces resulted in their popularity, not the least of which include limited medical knowledge, empirical advances in chemistry, and the inclination of the nineteenth-century mind for innovation. At army posts in the West, pharmacies were unknown, physicians were busy, and the environment was harsh. The result led to uninhibited consumption of patent medicine.

Much has been made of the high alcoholic content of these concoctions, and no doubt some were purchased by individuals who felt it necessary, for a variety of reasons, to disguise their desire for spiritous beverages. But it would be a mistake to assume that this was a universal attitude, particularly at the army posts. The human condition at these forts was subjected to stresses in excess of those in the settled areas of the country. The climate was particularly severe; life was, by its nature, physically strenuous; and sanitation was excessively primitive. While army posts were peopled by the young and healthy, conditions were sufficiently rigorous to produce a plethora of fevers and aches.

The army surgeon, to whom most personnel at a post had access, was no more skilled than his civilian counterpart and frequently was either a failure in private practice or sufficiently worn down by the overwork and small rewards of army service to have lost interest in, and dedication to, his profession. Under these conditions, individuals with less than mortal afflictions were attracted to patent medicines for relief.

As with most other bottles recovered at Fort Union and Fort Laramie, paper labels are almost wholly absent on these medicine bottles. Many, however, were made expressly for particular firms and can be identified by inscriptions molded in the glass. Many bottles, lacking labels or molded inscriptions, were arbitrarily classed as medicine containers because they closely resembled modern or historic types or because they contained residues indicative of medical preparations.

Here are several examples of advertisements for proprietary medicines:

AYER'S SARSAPARILLA

There is no excuse for those who drag their weary and disordered bodies into our company, when a few doses of Ayer's Sarsaparilla would cleanse their murky blood and restore their health and vigor. Ye muddy victims of bilious disease, have some regard for your neighbors, if not for yourselves.
— *Harper's Bazaar*, 1871.

The Chamberlain Company claimed that their Pain Balm was widely known as a cure for rheumatism, sprains and bruises (The State Register of Guthrie, Oklahoma, October 10, 1901).

DAVIS' PAIN KILLER

One teaspoonful of Perry Davis' Pain Killer in a little sweetened water or milk (hot if convenient), will immediately relieve any case of dysentery, cholera morbus, summer complaint or diarrhoea. If taken in time, one dose generally does the business; otherwise repeat at short intervals, and a speedy cure will follow. Pain Killer is equally effective in killing pain from cuts, bruises, bites, and burns, and no prudent person should fail to keep it by him. At all medicine dealers.
—*The Washington Post*, 1891.

An advertisement that appeared in *The Washington Post* in 1890 claimed that Ely's Cream Balm would cure catarrh, hay fever, and a cold in the head. A bottle retailed for 50 cents.

HAGAN'S MAGNOLIA BALM

Ladies do you want a pure, blooming complexion? If so, a few applications of Hagan's Magnolia Balm will gratify you to your heart's content. It does away with sallowness, redness, pimples, blotches, and all diseases and imperfections of the skin. It overcomes the flushed appearance of heat, fatigue and excitement. It makes a lady of thirty appear twenty; and so natural, gradual, and perfect are its effects, that it is impossible to detect its application.
—*The Saint Paul and Minneapolis Pioneer Press*, 1883.

JAYNE'S BALSAM

Jayne's Carminative Balsam, for bowel and summer complaints, colics, cholera morbus, and inflammation of the bowels.
—*The United Service*, September 1881.
This article was sold as early as 1831.

JAYNE'S EXPECTORANT

It is altogether wrong to trifle with a bad cough or cold, when the risk is so great and a remedy so sure, prompt, and thorough as Dr. Jayne's Expectorant can be readily found.
—*New York Daily Tribune*, April 26, 1873.
This product was on the market as early as 1842.

An advertisement appeared in *The Sioux City Journal* on September 13, 1892, which claimed that Dr. King's New Discovery for Consumption was also good for coughs, colds, etc., and that large size bottles sold for 50 cents and $1.

MEXICAN MUSTANG LINIMENT

The enemy of disease! The foe of pain to man and beast is the grand old Mustang Liniment, which has stood the test 40 years. There is no sore it will not cure, no ache, no pain, that affects the human body, or the body of a horse or other domestic animals, that does not yield to its magic touch. A bottle costing 25¢, or 50¢, or $, has often saved the life of a human being and restored to life. . . .
—*New York Daily Tribune*, April 26, 1873.

COMPOUND EXTRACT OF SMART-WEED

Dr. R. V. Pierce, of the World's Dispensary, Buffalo, N. Y., whose Family Medicines have won golden opinions and achieved world-wide reputation, after patient study and much experimenting, succeeded in perfecting a COMPOUND EXTRACT OF SMART-WEED, or WATER-PEPPER, that is destined to become as celebrated as his other medicines. It owes its efficacy not entirely to the smart-weed, which, however, is a sovereign remedial agent, but largely to a happy combination of that herb with Jamaica Ginger and other vegetable agents. The combination is such as to make it a very pleasant remedy to take. Taken internally, it cures diarrhoea, dysentery, (or bloody flux), summer complaint, cholera, cholera morbus, colic, cramps and pain in the stomach, breaks up colds, febrile and inflammatory attacks. It is sold by all druggists and dealers in medicines.
—*Harper's Weekly*, 1875.

PIERCE'S GOLDEN MEDICAL DISCOVERY

Symptoms of liver complaint. A sallow or yellow color of skin, or yellowish brown spots on face and other parts of body; dullness and drowsiness, with frequent headache; dizziness, bitter or bad taste in mouth, dryness of throat and internal heat; palpitation; in many cases a dry, teasing cough, with sore throat; unsteady appetite, raising of full feeling about stomach and sides, pain in sides, back, or breast, and about shoulders; colic, pain and soreness through bowels, with heat; constipation alternating with diarrhoea; piles, flatulence, nervousness, coldness of extremities; rush of blood to head, with symptoms of apoplexy, numbness of limbs, especially at night; cold chills alternating with hot flashes, kidney and urinary difficulties; dullness, low spirits, unsociability, and gloomy forebodings. Only a few of above symptoms likely to be present at one time. All who use Dr. Pierce's Alt. Ext., or Golden Medical Discovery for liver complaint and its complications are loud in its praise.
—*Harper's Weekly*, 1874.

CASTORIA

Pitcher's Castoria is not narcotic. Children grow fat upon, mothers like, and physicians recommend Castoria. It regulates the bowels, cures wind colic, allays feverishness, and destroys worms.
—*The Evening Express*, Los Angeles, 1881.

RADWAY'S READY RELIEF

Radway's Ready Relief cures the worst pains in from one to twenty minutes. Not one hour. After reading this advertisement, need any one suffer with pain? Radway's Ready Relief is a cure for every pain. It was first and is the only pain remedy. . .etc., etc. Fifty cents per bottle.
—*The Chicago Weekly*, 1880.

DR. SAGE'S CATARRH REMEDY

Symptoms of catarrh. Obstruction of nasal passages, discharge falling into throat; sometimes profuse, watery, acrid, or thick and tenacious, mucous, purulent, bloody, putrid, offensive, etc. In others a dryness, weak or inflamed eyes, ringing in ears, deafness, ulcerations, scabs from ulcers, voice altered, nasal twang, offensive breath, impaired smell and taste, etc. Few only of above symptoms likely to be present in any case at one time. To cure—take DR. PIERCE'S GOLDEN MEDICAL DISCOVERY earnestly, to correct the blood and system, which are always at fault, also to act specifically, as it does, upon the diseased glands and lining membrane of the nose and its communicating chambers. The more positive is my belief that if we would make treatment perfectly successful in curing it, we must use constitutional treatment to act through the blood as well as a soothing and healing local application. DR. SAGE'S CATARRH REMEDY, when used warm and applied with DR. PIERCE'S NASAL DOUCHE, effects cures upon commonsense, rational, and scientific principles, by its mild, soothing, and healing properties, to which the disease gradually yields, when the system has been put in perfect order by the use of the GOLDEN MEDICAL DISCOVERY. This is the only perfectly safe, scientific, and successful mode of acting upon and healing it. DISCOVERY, CATARRH REMEDY, and DOUCHE are sold by dealers in medicines the world over.

—*Harper's Weekly*, 1875.

ST. JACOBS OIL

Capital comfort. Washington, D. C.—Mrs. Mary K. Shoed, 1110 Maryland Avenue, Washington, D. C., states that for several years she had suffered terribly with facial neuralgia and could find no relief. In a recent attack which extended to the neck, shoulders, and back the pain was intense. She resolved to try St. Jacobs Oil, the great pain reliever. Rubbing the parts afflicted, three times only, all pain vanished as if by magic, and has not returned.

—*The Weekly Inter Ocean*, Chicago, 1885.

SWAIM'S CELEBRATED PANACEA

Swaim's Celebrated Panacea has attracted the notice of the most eminent and leading members of the medical profession in this country and Europe by its great power and excellence in curing what were considered incurable cases of disease where the patient had been almost destroyed by scrofula, &c., and Prof. Valentine Mott, of the New York University, Professors Gibson, Dewees and Chapman, of Philadelphia, and many other physicians of celebrity and eminence gave, over their own signatures, letters recommending it, and certifying to its great merits. It has been occasionally advertised during this long period, and thousands of families throughout the United States recommend and use it. The laboratory is under the direction of Dr. Franklin Stewart, who had devoted his attention and skill in its careful preparation during the past twenty-five years, and not a bottle is put up that is not worth ten times its full value to the patient. It is perfectly safe for the most diseased and debilitated, and will always relieve where it will not cure. In all cases where the blood is not pure it should be used freely. Prepared only at Swaim's Laboratory, 113 South Seventh St., below Chestnut St., Philadelphia. W. H. Schieffelin & Co., General Agents, 170 William Street, New York.

—*Harper's Weekly*, 1873.

TARRANT'S EFFERVESCENT SELTZER APERIENT

A harvest of diamonds has rewarded the toil of certain lucky adventurers under the burning sun of Africa; but what is the value of the rarest gem that ever glittered in crown or turban when compared with that of a medicinal remedy that cures dyspepsia and biliousness, restores the appetite, regulates the disordered bowels, and tones and invigorates the whole vital system? Science has bestowed upon the world this estimable gift in TARRANT'S EFFERVESCENT SELTZER APERIENT, which is to all other preparations of its class what the diamond is among jewels and, when foaming in the goblet of the fevered invalid, as bright and sparkling. Sold by all druggists.

—Harper's Bazaar, 1872.

TRASK'S MAGNETIC OINTMENT

DR. TRASK'S MAGNETIC OINTMENT contains no mineral. Its penetrating power is such that internal affections, like kidney, liver, bowel and lung complaints, yield as quickly as surface inflammations. 25 cts & 40 cts.

—The Evening Express, Los Angeles, 1881.

HORSFORD'S ACID PHOSPHATE

HORSFORD'S ACID PHOSPHATE for dyspepsia, mental and physical exhaustion, nervousness, diminished vitality, urinary difficulties, etc. Prepared according to the directions of Prof. E. N. Horsford, of Cambridge, Mass. There seems to be no difference of opinion in high medical authority of the value of phosphoric acid, and no preparation has ever been offered to the public which seems to so happily meet the general want as this. It is not nauseous, but agreeable to the taste. No danger can attend its use. Its action will harmonize with such stimulants as are necessary to take. It makes a delicious drink with water and sugar only. Horsford's Acid Phosphate is manufactured by the Rumford Chemical Works, Providence, R. I. Prices Reasonable.

—Standard Household Remedies, 1881.

HORSFORD'S ACID PHOSPHATE

How to preserve the teeth. It is not generally known that the teeth contain a larger proportion of phosphate of lime than any other part of the human body, and that it exists in a still greater quantity in the enamel than even in the tooth substance. This has, however, been proven by a great German chemist. Hence, phosphate of lime is indispensable to preserve the teeth, and HORSFORD'S ACID PHOSPHATE supplies this element in the most proper form. Send for free pamphlet, to H. M. Anthony, General Agent, 51 Murray Street, New York.

—Harper's Weekly, 1873.

100 **101**

100 Medicine bottle. Sarsaparilla panel, hood style. Transparent, light-blue glass. The neck finish has a double rounded collar. Molded with an inscription on a rectangular body: "AYER'S / COMPOUND EXT / LOWELL / MASS USA / SARSAPARILLA". Centered in the base is the number "10". Height, 8 1/2 inches; base, 2 3/4 × 1 5/8 inches. Capacity, about 7 ounces. Fort Union, 1865–90.

101 Medicine bottle. Transparent, colorless glass with a thickened, plain-lip neck finish. Molded with an inscription on a rectangular body: "SYRUP OF FIGS / CALIFORNIA FIG SYRUP CO / SAN FRANCISCO CAL / SYRUP OF FIGS." This type also occurred with the letter "B" inscribed in the center of the base and with slightly different base measurements. Height, 6 5/8 inches; base, 2 1/8 × 1 7/16 inches. Capacity, about 7 ounces. Fort Union, 1875–90.

102 Medicine bottle. Sarsaparilla panel, hood style. Transparent, light-blue glass. The neck finish has a double rounded collar and a double ring lip. Molded with an inscription on a rectangular body: "AYER'S / COMPOUND EXT. / LOWELL / MASS. U.S.A. / SAR-SAPARILLA". Centered in the base is the number "35". Ayer bottles from Fort Union were discarded there between 1865 and 1890 but the product continued to be sold after that time. Height, 8 1/2 inches; base, 2 3/4 × 1 3/4 inches. Capacity, about 12 ounces. Fort Union, 1865–90.

103 Medicine bottle. Plain, oval style. Transparent, light-blue glass with a thickened, plain-lip neck finish. Molded with an inscription on its flask-shaped body: "BROWN MED. & MFG. CO. / LEAVENWORTH / KAS." Height, 5 1/2 inches; base, 2 1/4 × 1 1/4 inches. Capacity, about 5 ounces. Fort Union, 1865–90.

102 103

104 Medicine bottle. Transparent, colorless glass with a flanged-lip neck finish. Molded with an inscription on a cylindrical body: "CHESEBROUGH MFG CO / VASELINE". Concave base has two raised dots. Height, 2 1/4 inches; base diameter, 1 9/16 inches. Capacity, about 1 ounce. Fort Union, 1865–90.

105 Medicine bottle. Transparent, colorless glass with a flanged-lip neck finish. Molded with an inscription on a cylindrical body: "CHESEBROUGH MFG Co / VASELINE". The letter "C" is centered in a concave base. An identical jar was also found at Fort Union with smaller lettering. Height, 2 7/8 inches; base diameter, 1 7/8 inches. Capacity, about 4 ounces. Fort Union, 1865–90.

104 105

106 Medicine bottle. Half panel style. Transparent, blue glass with a double ring lip and with a rounded-collar neck finish. Molded with an inscription on the broad side of the body that reads: "Davis". Inscribed on one narrow side is "VEGETABLE" with "PAIN KILLER" on the opposite side. Davis bottles sometimes appeared in colorless glass. Height, 4 7/8 inches; base, 1 7/16 × 3/4 inches. Capacity, about 2 ounces. Fort Union, 1851–90.

107 Medicine bottle. Short blake style. Transparent, amber glass with a plain neck finish. Molded with an inscription on a rectangular body: "ELY'S / CREAM / BALM / ELY BRO'S / OWEGO / N. Y. / CATARRH / HAY FEVER". Height, 2 5/8 inches; base, 1 5/16 × 15/16 inches. Capacity, about 3 ounces. Fort Union, 1865–90.

106 107

108

109

110

111

112

113

108 Medicine bottle. Transparent, light-blue glass with a broad, sloping-collar neck finish. Molded with an inscription on a paneled, rectangular body: "J. N. HARRIS & C⁰ / ALLEN'S / LUNG / BALSAM / CINCINNATI." Height, 7 5/8 inches; base, 2 3/4 × 1 1/2 inches. Capacity, about 11 ounces. Fort Union, 1865–90.

109 Medicine bottle. Transparent, light-blue glass with a thickened, plain-lip neck finish. Molded with an inscription on a rectangular body: "Dʀ D JAYNE'S / EXPECTORANT / PHILᴬ". Height, 7 inches; base, 1 5/8 × 2 1/2 inches. Capacity, about 12 ounces. Fort Union, 1870–90.

110 Medicine bottle. Ginger panel style. Transparent, light-blue glass with a double ring lip and with a rounded-collar neck finish. Molded with an inscription on a rectangular, paneled body: "H.E. BUCKLEN & Co. / Dʀ KING'S / NEW DISCOVERY / FOR CONSUMPTION / CHICAGO ILL." Height, 6 5/8 inches; base, 2 1/4 × 1 3/16 inches. Capacity, about 4 ounces. Fort Union, 1865–90.

111 Medicine bottle. Homeopathic vial. Transparent, colorless glass with a thickened, plain-lip neck finish. Molded with an inscription on a cylindrical body: "DR AUGUST KOENIGS / HAMBURGER / TROPFEN." Height, 3 3/4 inches; base diameter, 1 inch. Capacity, about 1 ounce. Fort Union, 1865–90.

112 Medicine bottle. Emulsion panel style. Transparent, colorless glass with a thickened, plain-lip neck finish. Molded with an inscription on a rectangular body: "P. R. LANCE & Co / NEW YORK / SPARKLING / APERIENT." Centered in the base are the inscribed letters "W. MᶜC. & CO". Height, 6 inches; base, 2 1/2 × 1 9/16 inches. Capacity, about 8 ounces. Fort Union, 1865–90.

113 Medicine bottle. Druggist's packing-bottle style. Transparent, light-blue glass with a thickened, plain-lip neck finish. Molded with an inscription on a cylindrical body: "MALLINCKRODT / CHEMICAL WORKS / ST. LOUIS". Height, 7 3/8 inches; base diameter, 2 7/8 inches. Capacity, about 17 ounces. Fort Union, 1882–90.

114 Medicine bottle. Narrow mouth; round, prescription style. Transparent, blue glass with a thickened, plain-lip neck finish. Blown-molded with an inscription on a cylindrical body: "MEXICAN / MUSTANG / LINIMENT / D•S•BARNES / N. Y." A rough pontil mark appears in the center of its concave base. Height, 4 inches; base diameter, 1 1/2 inches. Capacity, about 3 ounces. Fort Union, 1849–65.

115 Medicine bottle. Round, prescription style with a narrow mouth. Transparent, colorless glass with a thickened, plain-lip neck finish. Molded with inscription on cylindrical body: "MEXICAN / MUSTANG / LINIMENT / LYON MF'G C (O) / NEW YORK." Height, 3 3/4 inches; base diameter, unknown. Capacity, about 2 ounces. Fort Union, 1865–90.

114   115

116 Medicine bottle. Homeopathic vial. Transparent, light-blue glass with a thickened, plain-lip neck finish. Molded with an inscription on a cylindrical body: "D^R McMUNN'S / ELIXIR OF OPIUM." Several bottles of this type were recovered in close proximity to an unlined privy at the site of Sutler's Store at Fort Union. Height, 4 3/8 inches; base diameter, 15/16 inch. Capacity, about 1 ounce. Fort Union, 1880–90.

117 Medicine bottle. Cod liver oil panel style. Transparent, amber glass with a broad, sloping-collar neck finish. Molded with an inscription on a rectangular body: "PHILLIPS' EMULSION / COD-LIVER OIL / NEW YORK". Height, 9 3/8 inches; base, 3 1/4 × 2 7/8 inches. Capacity, about 16 ounces. Fort Union, 1865–90.

116   117

118 Medicine bottle. Union, oval style prescription bottle. Transparent, blue glass with a thickened, plain-lip neck finish. Molded with an inscription on its flask-shaped body: "PRESCRIBED / BY / R. V. PIERCE MD / BUFFALO / N. Y." inside a circle. Height, 6 7/8 inches; base, 2 3/4 × 1 5/8 inches. Capacity, about 8 ounces. Fort Union, 1870–90.

119 Medicine bottle. Ginger panel style. Transparent, light-blue glass with a broad, sloping-collar neck finish. Molded with an inscription on a rectangular body: "DR PIERCE'S / GOLDEN MEDICAL DISCOVERY / BUFFALO N. Y. / R. V. PIERCE MD". Centered in the base is inscribed the number "4". Height, 7 3/4 inches; base, 2 7/8 × 1 1/2 inches. Capacity, about 10 ounces. Fort Union, 1865–90.

118   119

120

121

120   Medicine bottle. Ginger panel style.
Transparent, light-blue glass with a double,
rounded-collar neck finish. Molded with an
inscription on a rectangular body: "DR. / S.
PITCHER'S / CASTORIA." Centered in base
is number "16". Height, 5 3/4 inches; base,
2 × 1 inches. Capacity, about 4 ounces.
Fort Union, 1865–90.

121   Medicine bottle. Ball-neck panel style.
Transparent, blue glass with a thickened,
plain-lip neck finish. Molded with an inscription on a rectangular body: "RENNE'S /
NERVINE". Height, 6 1/8 inches; base, 2 1/8×
1 1/16 inches. Capacity, about 5 ounces.
Fort Union, 1865–90.

122

123

122   Medicine bottle. Transparent, light-blue
glass with a broad, sloping-collar neck finish.
Molded with an inscription on a paneled, rectangular body: "SCOVILL / BLOOD & /
LIVER SYRUP / CINCINNATI O." Height, 9 1/4
inches; base, 2 7/8 × 1 5/8 inches. Capacity,
about 13 ounces. Fort Union, 1865–90.

**123   Medicine bottle. Wide mouth; round,
prescription style.** Transparent, green glass
with a flanged lip and a glass-stopper neck
finish. Molded with an inscription around the
shoulder: "E. R. SQUIBB." Height, 7 1/8 inches;
base diameter, 3 1/8 inches. Capacity, about
19 ounces. Fort Union, 1865–90.

124

125

**124   Medicine bottle. Narrow mouth, Boston
prescription style.** Transparent, green glass
with a prescription lip and a glass-stopper
neck finish. Molded with an inscription around
the shoulder: "E. R. SQUIBB." May have contained acid or tincture. Height, 4 7/8 inches;
base diameter, 1 7/8 inches. Capacity, about
7 ounces. Fort Union, 1865–90.

**125   Medicine bottle. Wide mouth, Boston
prescription style.** Transparent, blue glass
with a prescription lip and a glass-stopper
neck finish. Molded with an inscription around
the shoulder: "E. R. SQUIBB." Height, 5 3/4
inches; base diameter, 2 3/8 inches. Capacity,
about 11 ounces. Fort Union, 1865–90.

126 Medicine bottle. Transparent, light-blue glass with double, rounded-collar neck finish. Molded with an inscription on a cylindrical body: "ST. JAKOBS OEL / A VOGELER & Co. / BALTIMORE, MD." Centered in concave base is inscribed letter "L". Height, 6 3/8 inches; base diameter, 1 1/2 inches. Capacity, about 5 ounces. Fort Union, 1865–80.

127 Medicine bottle. Transparent, green glass with a narrow ring beneath a broad, sloping-collar neck finish. Made in a wooden mold, with an inscription on a paneled, fluted, cylindrical body: "PHILADᴬ / SWAIM'S / PANACEA". Height, 7 1/8 inches; base diameter, 3 1/2 inches. Capacity, about 24 ounces. Fort Union, 1865–90.

126

127

128 Medicine bottle. Transparent, colorless glass with a thickened, plain-lip neck finish. Molded with an inscription on a rectangular body: "TARRANT & CO / DRUGGISTS / NEW YORK". Height, 5 3/16 inches; base, 2 1/2 × 1 1/2 inches. Capacity, about 8 ounces. Fort Union, 1865–90.

129 Medicine bottle. Wide mouth; French, square, prescription style. Transparent, light-blue glass with a prescription-lip neck finish. Molded with an inscription on a rectangular body: "TRASKS / MAGNETIC / OINT-MENT." Height, 2 5/8 inches; base, 1 1/4 × 1 1/4 inches. Capacity, about 2 ounces. Fort Union, 1865–90.

128

129

130 Medicine bottle. Transparent, amber glass with a flanged-lip neck finish. Molded, pear-shaped body, with the inscription: "VALENTINE'S / MEAT JUICE". This product was considered medicinal and was not, as might be assumed, used for culinary purposes. Height, 3 1/8 inches; base diameter, 1 3/16 inches. Capacity, about 3 ounces. Fort Union, 1871–90.

131 Medicine bottle. Transparent, colorless glass with a flanged-lip neck finish. Molded with a large "W" inside a circle inscribed on the cylindrical body. Height, 3 1/4 inches; base diameter, 2 1/4 inches. Capacity, about 6 ounces. Fort Union, 1865–90.

130

131

132

133

132 Medicine bottle. Transparent, colorless glass with a thickened, plain-lip neck finish. A molded inscription on the shoulder reads: "H. T. & Co." This product may have been used for a chemical. Height 5 1/4 inches; base diameter, 2 5/8 inches. Capacity, about 10 ounces. Fort Union, 1863–90.

133 Medicine bottle. Transparent, colorless glass with a thickened, plain-lip neck finish. Height, 2 1/4 inches; base, 3/4 × 1 inch. Capacity, about 1 ounce. Fort Union, 1865–90.

134

135

134 Medicine bottle. Flat, paneled, oval style. Transparent, colorless glass with a prescription-lip neck finish. Height, 2 7/8 inches × 1 1/4 inches. Capacity, about 1 ounce. Fort Union, 1870–90.

135 Medicine bottle. Wide mouth, round style. Transparent, green glass with thickened, plain-lip neck finish. Molded with "C B / M / 630" in base. Height, 8 inches; base diameter, 4 1/8 inches. Capacity, about 40 ounces. Fort Union, 1863–90.

136

137

136 Medicine bottle. Paneled, square style. Transparent, colorless glass with a prescription-lip neck finish. Molded with an inscription on the body: "VAN SCHAACK / STEVENSON & CO / CHICAGO". Inscribed in the center of the base is the letter "R". Height, 4 1/8 inches; base, 1 3/8 × 1 3/8 inches. Capacity, about 3 ounces. Fort Union, 1865–90.

137 Medicine bottle. Plain, oval style. Transparent, colorless glass with a prescription-lip neck finish. Molded. Height, 2 3/4 inches; base, 5/8 × 1 1/4 inches. Capacity, about 1 ounce. Fort Union, 1865–90.

138 Medicine bottle. Transparent, blue glass. Molded with an inscription on the body: "ST JAKOBS OEL / A VOGELER & Co / BALTIMORE MD." The center of the base is inscribed with the number "5". This bottle seems to be identical with No. 126 from Fort Union except for the base marking and a difference in the size of letters of the body inscription. Height, unknown; base diameter, 1 3/8 inches. Capacity, about 5 ounces. Fort Union, 1865–90.

139 Medicine bottle. Transparent, blue glass with a prescription-lip neck finish. Molded. Height, 3 5/8 inches; base diameter, 1 1/2 inches. Capacity, about 3 ounces. Fort Union, 1865–90.

138   139

140 Medicine bottle. Transparent, colorless glass with a prescription-lip neck finish. Molded. Height, 3 inches; base diameter, 3/4 inch. Capacity, about 1 ounce. Fort Union, 1870–90.

141 Medicine bottle. Transparent, colorless glass with a bead neck finish. Molded with an inscription on the body: "CHESEBROUGH MFG Co / VASELINE". This specimen is similar to No. 105, except for the size of the lettering. Height, 2 7/8 inches; base diameter, 1 7/8 inches. Capacity, about 4 ounces. Fort Union, 1865–90.

140   141

142 Medicine bottle. Transparent, colorless glass with a prescription-lip neck finish. Molded. Height, 2 5/8 inches; base diameter, 1 3/8 inches. Capacity, about 2 ounces. Fort Union, 1870–90.

143 Medicine bottle. Transparent, colorless glass with a prescription-lip neck finish. Molded with an inscription on the body: "WYETH & BRO / PHILA PA". Height, 3 5/16 inches; base, 1 × 1 7/16 inches. Capacity, about 2 ounces. Fort Union, 1875–90.

142   143

144

145

144 Medicine bottle. Union, oval style. Transparent, colorless glass with a prescription-lip neck finish. Molded. Height, 4 1/2 inches; base, 1 5/8×2 inches. Capacity, about 5 ounces. Fort Union, 1880–90.

145 Medicine bottle. Transparent, blue glass with a ring-lip neck finish and with a narrow ring beneath. Molded with an inscription on the body: "ACT OF CONGRESS / R.R.R./ RADWAY & CO. / NEW YORK / ENT$^{\underline{D}}$ ACOR$^{\underline{D}}$TO." Height, 6 inches; base, 3 inches × 13/16 inch. Capacity, about 2 1/2 ounces. Fort Union, 1865–90.

146

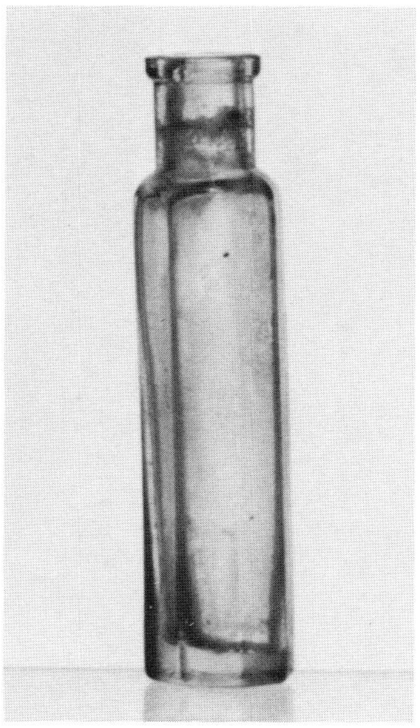

147

146 Medicine bottle. Transparent, blue glass with a ring-lip neck finish and with a narrow ring beneath. Molded with an inscription on the body: "M$^{\underline{C}}$LEANS / VOLCANIC / OIL / LINIMENT". Height, 4 inches; base, 1 1/4 × 1 1/4 inches. Capacity, about 1 ounce. Fort Union, 1865–90.

147 Medicine bottle. Homeopathic vial (?). Transparent, blue glass with a thickened, plain-lip neck finish. Molded. Height, 3 3/4 inches; diameter of octagonal base, 7/8 inch. Capacity, about 1 ounce. Fort Union, 1865–80.

148

149

148 Medicine bottle. Transparent, colorless glass with a prescription-lip neck finish. Molded. The remnants of the paper labels read: "G. . .LDINE / . . . on of Sandalwood / . . .E BEFORE USING. / CHARLE. . .GHT & CO., / Manufacturing Pharmacists, / DETROIT MICH. / DIRECTI. . . / THE CIRCULAR ACCOMPANYING THIS PREPARATION GIVES DETAILED / DIRECTIONS AS TO USING. THIS LABEL CAN BE REMOVED BY PLACING / THE BOTTLE IN WARM WATER, THEREBY AVOIDING DETECTION, IF SAME IS / DESIRED." Height, 5 9/16 inches; base, 1 3/4 × 1 3/4 inches. Capacity, about 6 ounces. Fort Union, 1880–90.

149 Medicine bottle. Transparent, colorless glass with a prescription-lip neck finish. Molded. Centered in the base is "R. D. Co." Height, 4 1/4 inches; base, 1 × 1 3/4 inches. Capacity, about 3 ounces. Fort Union, 1875–90.

150 Medicine (?) bottle. Wide mouth, pre-scription style with a ring lip. Transparent, colorless glass with a narrow-collar neck finish. Molded with the letters "H T & CO" inside a diamond-shaped enclosure on a cylindrical body. Height, 2 5/8 inches; base diameter, 1 1/4 inches. Capacity, about 1 ounce. Fort Union, 1865–90.

151 Medicine (?) bottle. Short blake style with a ring lip. Transparent, colorless glass with a flanged-lip neck finish. Molded with the letters "L M & G" inscribed on the rectangular body. Height, 3 5/8 inches; base, 1 3/4 × 1 1/4 inches. Capacity, about 2 ounces. Fort Union, 1865–90.

150   151

152 Medicine (?) bottle. Transparent, color-less glass with a flanged-lip neck finish. Molded with an inscription on the flask-shaped body: "ROCHESTER / CHEMICAL / WORKS". Height, 3 3/4 inches; base, 2 1/4 × 1 3/8 inches. Capacity, about 5 ounces. Fort Union, 1865–90.

153 Medicine (?) bottle. Transparent, color-less glass; prescription style with a narrow, rounded-collar neck finish. Molded with an in-scription inside a circle on a cylindrical body: "JAMES P. SMITH / NEW YORK / CHICAGO." Height, 5 3/4 inches; base diameter, 2 inches. Capacity, about 8 ounces. Fort Union, 1865–90.

152   153

154 Medicine (?) bottle. Transparent, green glass with a thickened, plain-lip neck finish. Molded in the center of the base is the letter "K". Height, 5 1/8 inches; base diameter, 3 1/8 inches. Capacity, about 15 ounces. Fort Union, 1865–90.

155 Medicine (?) bottle. Transparent, pale blue glass with a prescription-lip neck finish. Height, 2 3/4 inches; base diameter, 1 inch. Capacity, about 1 ounce. Fort Union, 1865–90.

154   155

156

157

156 Medicine (?) bottle. Transparent, colorless glass with a flaring neck finish. Molded. The base is marked in the center with an anchor and fouled line. Height, 4 3/8 inches; base diameter, 2 7/8 inches. Capacity, about 13 ounces. Fort Union, 1863–90.

157 Medicine (?) bottle. Transparent, colorless glass with a thickened, plain-lip neck finish. Blown-molded. The base is marked by a pontil scar. Height, 2 1/2 inches; base diameter, 1 1/4 inches. Capacity, about 2 ounces. Fort Union, 1860–65.

158

159

158 Medicine (?) bottle. Transparent, paneled, colorless glass with a prescription-lip neck finish and a rounded ring at the base of the neck. Molded with "902" in the center of the base. Height, 3 5/8 inches; base, 1 3/4 × 1 1/4 inches. Capacity, about 4 ounces. Fort Union, 1875–90.

159 Medicine (?) bottle. Transparent, blue glass with a thickened, plain-lip neck finish. Molded. Height, 3 1/2 inches; base, 1 1/2 × 1 1/2 inches. Capacity, about 4 ounces. Fort Union, 1865–90.

160

161

160 Medicine bottle. Transparent, light-green glass with a broad, sloping-collar neck finish. Molded with an inscription on a rectangular body: "CHAMBERLAIN / CHAMBERLAIN'S / COLIC AND / DIARRHOEA REMEDY / BOTTLE MADE IN U.S.A." The number "3" occurs in the center of the base. Height, 4 1/2 inches; base, 1 3/4 × 7/8 inches. Capacity, about 2 ounces. Fort Laramie, 1880–90.

161 Medicine bottle. Transparent, light-green glass with a broad, sloping-collar neck finish. Molded with an inscription on a rectangular body: "CHAMBERLAIN, MED. Co. / CHAMBERLAIN'S / COLIC AND / DIARRHOEA REMEDY / DES MOINES. IA. U.S.A." The number "3" is inscribed in the center of the base. Height, 4 5/8 inches; base, 1 3/4 × 7/8 inches. Capacity, about 2 ounces. Fort Laramie, 1885–90.

162 Medicine bottle. Transparent, light-blue glass with a broad, sloping-collar neck finish. Molded with an inscription on a rectangular body: "CHAMBERLAIN MED Co. / CHAMBER-LAIN'S / PAIN - BALM / DES MOINES, IA. U.S.A." Height, 7 inches; base, 2 3/8 × 1 5/16 inches. Capacity, about 7 ounces. Fort Laramie, 1885–90.

163 Medicine bottle. Transparent, colorless glass with a prescription-lip neck finish. Molded with an inscription on a rectangular body: "FRANCIS / BROS. / PROPRS / UHRICHSVILLE / OHIO." Height, 2 inches; base, 3/4 ×3/4 inch. Capacity, about 1/4 ounce. Fort Laramie, 1880–90.

162

163

164 Medicine bottle. Transparent, light-green glass with a broad, cylindrical-collar neck finish. Molded with an inscription on the body: "J.R. BURDSALL'S / ARNICA / LINIMENT / NEW YORK". The paper label reads, across the top: "BURDSALL'S / CELEBRATED / ARNICA / LINIMENT"; down the left side: "(picture of a man) / Rheumatism / Sprains / Pains in the / Back, Chest &c / Sore & Broken / Breast / Chilblains / Cramps / Burns & / Scalds / Bruises / Cuts and / Wounds / Sore Throat / Neuralgia / Swell'd Face"; down the right side: "(picture of a horse) / Ring Bone / Spavins / Chafes / Foundered Feet / Lameness / Contraction / of the Muscles / Mange / Strains / Wind Galls / Scratches / Crack'd Heels / Old Sores / Sit Fast / Chest Founder / Poll Evil"; down the center: "DIRECTIONS / In all ordinary cases / this Liniment can be ap / plied with the bare hand / or flannel at any time & / as often as convenient. / BURNS, SCALDS, CHILBLAINS / cuts and any wound wh / ere the skin is broken ap- / ply the Liniment with a / feather or saturate pieces / of linen and lay or bind / on the injured parts. / This invaluable Oleogenous / Liniment acts like Magic in / removing the most acute pain / and seldom requires but one / application to cure every kind / of external Complaint." Across the bottom of the label reads: "Sold by Druggists & Agents throughout the United States & Canadas / J.R. Burdsall / Copyright Secured 1849 NEW YORK". Height, 5 9/16 inches; base, 2 5/16 inches × 1 inch. Capacity, about 3 ounces. Fort Laramie, 1880–90.

164

165 Medicine bottle. Transparent, colorless glass with a thin, crude, prescription-lip neck finish. Blown-molded with an inscription on a cylindrical body: "DR D. JAYNE'S / CARMINA-TIVE / BALSAM / PHILAD^A". A pontil mark appears in the center of a concave base. Height, 4 3/4 inches; base diameter, 1 1/8 inches. Capacity, about 2 ounces. Fort Laramie, 1849–65.

165

166

166 Medicine bottle. Transparent, colorless glass with a prescription-lip neck finish. Molded with an inscription on a paneled, rectangular body: "DR T. A. Dutton. / NEW BRUNSWICK, / N. J. / VEGETABLE / DISCOVERY". Paper label remnant reads: "_____ / . . . iscovery / . . . ier. / . . . tomach, / _____ / Liver Co. _____ / _____ / $1.00, . . . spoon / . . . -ter eat- / _____ adult, if / constip. . . bowels take / five dr. . . move bowels / once _____ you can / be . . . ing. _____ . . . owels move / too freely . . . s, but / don. . . stop entire. . . / _____ incre. . . movements are sluggish. / H.L. LANCHILD (?) / NEW BRUNSWICK, N. J., SOLE PROPRIETOR". Height, 6 inches; base, 2 5/16 × 1 3/8 inches. Capacity, about 4 ounces. Fort Laramie, 1865–90.

167

168

167 Medicine bottle. Transparent, light-green glass with a thickened, plain-lip neck finish. Molded with an inscription on a cylindrical body: "SAMPLE BOTTLE / DR KILMER'S / SWAMP ROOT KIDNEY CURE / BINGHAMTON N Y". The number "4" is inscribed in the center of the base. Height, 4 1/4 inches; base diameter, 1 1/16 inches. Capacity, about 2 ounces. Fort Laramie, 1885–90.

168 Medicine bottle. Wide mouth, French, square style. Transparent, light-blue glass with a narrow, rounded-collar neck finish. Molded with an inscription on a rectangular body: "DOCT / MARSHALL'S / SNUFF." Also found at Fort Union, this specimen probably contained Dr. Marshall's Catarrh Snuff. Height, 3 1/4 inches; base, 1 × 1 5/16 inches. Capacity, about 1 ounce. Fort Laramie, 1865–90.

169

170

169 Medicine bottle. Transparent, light-blue glass with a thickened, plain-lip neck finish. Molded with an inscription on a cylindrical body: "MEXICAN / MUSTANG / LINIMENT / LYON MFG. Co / NEW YORK." Height, 5 1/2 inches; base diameter, 2 1/16 inches. Capacity, about 6 1/2 ounces. Fort Laramie, 1865–90.

170 Medicine bottle. Transparent, light-blue glass with a thickened, plain-lip neck finish. Molded with an inscription on a cylindrical body: "MEXICAN / MUSTANG / LINIMENT / LYON MFG CO / NEW YORK." Height, 3 15/16 inches; base diameter, 1 1/2 inches. Capacity, about 3 ounces. Fort Laramie, 1865–90.

171 Medicine bottle. Transparent, colorless glass. Molded with an inscription on a rectangular body: "PARKE DAVIS & C⁰ / CHEMISTS / DETROIT". Height, 2 7/8 inches; base, 15/16 × 15/16 inches. Capacity, about 1 ounce. Fort Laramie, 1880–90.

172 Medicine bottle. Transparent, light-blue glass. Molded with an inscription on a rectangular body: "Dᴿ SAGES / CATARRH / REMEDY / BUFFALO / Dᴿ PIERCE / PROPR." Height, 2 3/16 inches; base 1 1/4 × 3/4 inches. Capacity, about 1 ounce. Fort Laramie, 1885–90.

171

172

173 Medicine bottle. Transparent, colorless glass with a thickened, plain-lip neck finish. Molded with an inscription on a rectangular body: "BOERICKE / & TAFEL". Height, 2 inches; base, 5/8 inch square. Capacity, about 1/8 ounce. Fort Laramie, 1880–90.

174 Medicine bottle. Transparent, colorless glass with a thickened, plain-lip neck finish. Molded. Height, 6 1/16 inches; base diameter, 2 3/16 inches. Capacity, about 6 ounces. Fort Laramie, 1870–90.

173

174

175 Medicine bottle. Transparent, light-blue glass with a double, rounded-collar neck finish. Molded with an inscription on a cylindrical body: "S⠐ Jakobs Oel / Das grosse Schmerzenheilmittlel / TRADE MARK / (Six lines of German text follow) / The Charles A. Vogeler Company, / Baltimore, M.D., U.S.A." Another St. Jakobs bottle was found at Fort Laramie which bears an Anglicized inscription that reads: "St. Jacobs oil, the great remedy for pain./NOTICE. St. Jacobs oil should be kept in a cool place, well corked, and never subjected to or applied near fire, flame or heat. / For all bodily pains apply St. Jacobs oil by thoroughly / rubbing over the affected region keeping well protected against / ...old. (For further external as also for internal use see specific directions, in all languages, given with each bottle. None / ...uine without the facsimile signature of the sole proprietors / ...re shown). / ...ee, in the / ...nited Stat..., 50 cents a bottle./ The Charles A. Vogeler Co / Baltimore, Maryland, U.S.A. / (Three lines of Spanish follow)". Height, 6 5/16 inches; base diameter, 1 3/8 inches. Capacity, about 4 ounces. Fort Laramie, 1865–80.

175

176

177

176 Medicine bottle. Transparent, colorless glass with a bead neck finish. Molded with an inscription on the body: "CHESEBROUGH MFG Co / VASELINE". Height, 2 15/16 inches; base diameter, 1 13/16 inches. Capacity, about 3 ounces. Fort Laramie, 1870–90.

177 Medicine bottle. This specimen is practically identical to No. 176, and probably contained petroleum. Remnant of the paper label reads: "_____ lin... / (several lines of illegible text) / Chese... _____".

178

179

178 Medicine bottle. Transparent, colorless glass with a thickened, plain-lip neck finish. Remnant of the paper label reads: "_____ / ...ANTEED PURE / WEIGH...MAN / _____ / _____". Height, 5 1/8 inches; base diameter, 2 1/16 inches. Capacity, about 8 ounces. Fort Laramie, 1870–90.

179 Medicine bottle. Transparent, colorless glass with a thickened, plain-lip neck finish. Molded. Paper label text: "ALCOHOL / ESTABLISHED 1867 / A & G / ADDOMS & GLOVER / DRUGGITS (sic) / Corner Sixteenth and Eddy Sts. / CHEYENNE, W. T." Height, 4 13/16 inches; base, 1 7/8 × 1 1/16 inches. Capacity, about 2 ounces. Fort Laramie, 1870–90.

180

181

180 Medicine bottle. Transparent, green glass with a thickened plain-lip neck finish. Molded. Broken, ground glass stopper in situ. Height, 5 7/8 inches; base diameter, 2 3/4 inches. Capacity, about 10 ounces. Fort Laramie, 1870–90.

181 Medicine bottle. Transparent, colorless glass with a thickened, plain-lip neck finish. Molded with an inscription on the body: "TARRANT & CO / DRUGGISTS / NEW YORK". Remnant of the paper label text reads: "_____ / that the properties of the ape... / ...ray contain himp, pur... / ..ases _____ to replace / the _____ after ...eing". The neck label reads, on one side: "To prev... / tarra... / rug..."; and on the other side of this neck label: "_____ / ... pany / _____ York". Height, 5 1/16 inches; base, 2 1/2 × 1 9/16 inches. Capacity, about 7 ounces. Fort Laramie, 1865–90.

182 Medicine bottle. Transparent, colorless glass with a thickened, plain-lip neck finish. Molded. Centered in the base is the number "75". Height, 4 1/8 inches; base diameter, 1 11/16 inches. Capacity, about 4 ounces. Fort Laramie, 1870–90.

183 Medicine bottle. Transparent, colorless glass with a thickened, plain-lip neck finish. Molded with an inscription on the body: "CHESEBROUGH / VASELINE / MAN-UFACT'G, CO." Centered in the base is an imperfectly molded letter "I" or numeral "1". Height, 3 5/8 inches; base diameter, 2 3/8 inches. Capacity, about 6 ounces. Fort Laramie, 1870–90.

182   183

184 Medicine bottle. Transparent, colorless glass with a thickened plain-lip neck finish. Molded. Height, 2 1/2 inches; base diameter, 1 1/2 inches. Capacity, about 2 ounces. Fort Laramie, 1870–90.

185 Medicine bottle. Transparent, colorless glass with a thickened, plain-lip neck finish. Molded with the letter "D" in the center of the base. Height, 5 3/16 inches; base diameter, 2 inches. Capacity, about 8 ounces. Fort Laramie, 1870–90.

184   185

186 Medicine bottle. Transparent, blue glass with a prescription-lip neck finish. Molded. Height, 6 1/4 inches; base diameter, 2 1/2 inches. Capacity, about 10 ounces. Fort Laramie, 1870–90.

187 Medicine bottle. Transparent, blue glass with a thickened, plain-lip neck finish. Molded. Height, 6 3/4 inches; base diameter, 2 13/16 inches. Capacity, about 15 ounces. Fort Laramie, 1870–90.

186   187

188

189

188 Medicine bottle. Transparent, blue glass with a broad sloping-collar neck finish and with a beveled ring beneath. Molded with an inscription on the body: "DR D. JAYNE'S / EXPECTORANT / PHILAD^A." Height, 7 1/8 inches; base 2 5/8 × 1 3/4 inches. Capacity, about 9 ounces. Fort Laramie, 1870–90.

189 Medicine bottle. Transparent, colorless glass with a prescription-lip neck finish. The body is flattened on one side, rounded on others. Molded with the inscription: "GEO. W. HOYT / PHARMACIST / CHEYENNE. W. T." Centered in the base are the inscribed letters "W. T. & Co" and centered directly below is the letter "B" facing left. Height, 6 5/8 inches; base, 2 11/16 × 1 11/16 inches. Capacity, about 9 ounces. Fort Laramie, 1870–89.

190

191

190 Medicine bottle. Transparent, colorless glass with a thickened, plain-lip neck finish. Molded with an inscription within panels on a rectangular body: "RAWLEIGH MED CO / RAWLEIGH'S / TRADE MARK / FREEPORT, ILL." Molded near the center of the base is the letter "R". Height, 6 1/4 inches; base, 2 5/16 × 1 1/4 inches. Capacity, about 5 ounces. Fort Laramie, 1880–90.

191 Chemical bottle. Fluted, prescription style. Transparent, blue glass with a flanged-lip neck finish. Molded with an inscription on two panels of the body: "RUMFORD / CHEMI-CAL WORKS" above and perpendicular to which is the letter "W". The octagonal, concave base has inscribed around its perimeter: "PATENTED / MARCH 10 1868." Height, 5 7/8 inches; base diameter, 2 1/2 inches. Capacity, about 10 ounces. Fort Union, 1868–90.

192

193

192 Medicine (?) bottle. Transparent, blue glass with a thickened, plain-lip neck finish. Molded with an inscription on the body: "DE LA COUR'S / BALM OF THE / WHITE WATER LILLY / CAMDEN, N. J." The text, much of which is illegible, on the remnant of the paper label begins: "EXTRACT / OF / JAMAICA (G)INGER / This Essence is..." and continues for 26 lines. Across the bottom of the label, separated from the above text: "_____ FROM / ...LA COUR, Chemist & D... / ...W....ar...d & Plum St., Camde... _____".

193 Chemical bottle. Transparent, green glass with a thickened, plain-lip neck finish. Molded. Height, 9 inches; base diameter, 3 9/16 inches. Capacity, about 35 ounces. Fort Laramie, 1870–90.

194 Narrow-mouth, druggists' packing bottle. Transparent, amber glass with a thickened, plain-lip neck finish. Molded with an inscription on its flask-shaped body: "...ARANTEE / STAMP / (two straight embossed lines with a dot between them) / CALVERT'S / EXTRA PURE / CARBOLIC / ACID". Above this description on the shoulder is a small wheel design flanked by arrow symbols pointed in each of four directions, all contained within a circle. The oval base is inscribed with a kite-shaped seal enclosing the letters "Y", "C", and "Co." Height, 7 7/8 inches; base, 3 3/8 × 2 1/4 inches. Capacity, unknown. Fort Union, 1865–90.

195 Chemical bottle. Transparent, colorless glass with a thickened, plain-lip neck finish. Molded. Height, 5 inches; base diameter, 2 5/8 inches. Capacity, about 10 ounces. Fort Laramie, 1870–90.

194

195

196 Chemical bottle. Transparent, colorless glass with a thickened, plain-lip neck finish. Molded with an inscription on the body: "M.A. SEED DRY PLATE CO / ST LOUIS MO." Height, 5 3/4 inches; base diameter, 2 1/4 inches. Capacity, about 10 ounces. Fort Union, 1865–90.

197 Hospital bottle. Transparent, colorless glass with a thickened plain-lip neck finish. Molded with an inscription on the body: "U.S.A. / HOSP DEPT." Height, 3 1/16 inches; base diameter, 1 5/16 inches. Capacity, about 2 ounces. Fort Laramie, 1870–90.

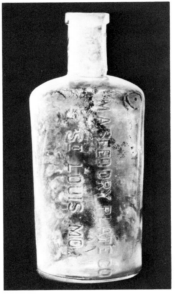

196

197

198 Hospital bottle. Transparent, colorless glass with a thin, flaring neck finish. Molded with an inscription on the body: "U. S. A. / HOSP. DEPT." Height, 4 3/16 inches; base diameter, 1 9/16 inches. Capacity, about 2 ounces. Fort Laramie, 1870–90.

199 Hospital bottle. Transparent, blue glass with a thickened, plain-lip neck finish. Molded with an inscription on the body: "U. S. A. / HOSP. DEPT." Height, 6 1/16 inches; base diameter, 2 7/16 inches. Capacity, about 11 ounces. Fort Laramie, 1870–90.

198

199

200

201

200 Medicine, perfume or extract bottle. Round, Lubin style with an inclined shoulder. Transparent, colorless glass with a flanged-lip neck finish. Molded with "HART" inscribed on a cylindrical body. Height, 2 1/2 inches; base diameter, 1 5/16 inches. Capacity, about 3 ounces. Fort Union, 1865–90.

201 Malt extract bottle. Transparent, light-blue glass. Neck finish type is unknown, but probably the broad-collar type designed for use with a patent stopper. Molded with an inscription on a cylindrical body: "JSP" interlocking in monogram fashion. Height, unknown; base diameter, 2 1/2 inches. Capacity, about 11 ounces. Fort Union, 1880–90.

For many centuries preparations designed to enhance human appearance have been compounded to lessen the disparity between realities and the changing view of how man wishes to appear. Toiletries were prized in the ancient Near East and Egypt as early as 3500 B.C. Their preparation was considered a mysterious art, and their use was often associated with religion. So closely does this tradition of the supernatural cling that the use of toiletries in Western civilization has been attended by violent peaks and valleys of acceptance and prohibition, coinciding with waves of secularism and religiosity. The 19th century in this country was a period of heavy superficial morality, and the use of cosmetics was frowned upon and confined to persons on the fringe of acceptable society.

That their use was not wholly avoided is attested by the numerous toiletry bottles found at Fort Union and Fort Laramie. The bottles are quite reflective of prevalent social attitudes. Many are patterned after medicine bottles, which suggests that the use of beauty preparations often masqueraded behind the pretext of medical need, a fact borne out by documentary evidence. Even with this justification, the variety of beauty aids in use at the posts does not appear to have been large. Lotions seem to have been common, as well as several preparations for care of the hair. The discovery of a bottle of hair dye, difficult to link to any health benefit, seems a bit remarkable in view of 19th-century social attitudes. It conjures up delightful visions of an army wife, or perhaps her husband, taking drastic action behind closed doors and blinds to deny the evidence of time.

By far the greatest number of cosmetic bottles at the two forts were those which contained perfume or cologne. Scents were in general use by women of the period, and their containers reflect a fascinating combination of attitudes.

Many perfume and cologne bottles found at the site bear a distinct resemblance to those which contained medicine. Thus, it would appear that even this oldest of beauty preparations did not escape the judgment of the 19th century. Indeed, the use of scents by many "gentle ladies" of the army was often justified as a medical measure, especially when used in combination with salts as an antidote for fainting, or on a handkerchief held to the nose as protection against impure air or vapors.

Other bottles indicate that some people wore perfume solely to enhance their attractiveness. These were made in the oldest tradition of cosmetic containers. It is worth noting that cosmetics were associated with special and sacred functions in ancient times and that their containers frequently were exquisite works of art. Most were pot or vase shaped, and made of precious materials such as alabaster, ivory, and onyx, carved in elegant forms. Handsome vase containers of glass were used in Egypt for kohl as early as the 4th century B.C. Beautiful containers are still used for toiletries, particularly for products associated with scent. Perfume bottles found at Forts Laramie and Union are notable for their elaborate designs and variety of form. This fact permits many bottles, otherwise unidentifiable, to be recognized as perfume or cologne containers simply because their elaborate design is in this ancient tradition. Such bottles could only have been used by 19th-century persons in an open effort to enhance their charms without medical pretext, and the romantic names for some of the compounds also attest to this fact.

Examples of toiletry articles are represented by the following advertisements:

BATCHELOR'S HAIR DYE

Batchelor's Celebrated Improved Hair Dye, which is warranted to change any colored hair to a glossy jet black or brown, instantaneously, without any injury to the skin.
—*The National Era*, Washington, D. C., 1854.

BATCHELOR'S HAIR DYE

Batchelor's Hair Dye is the best in the world—the only safe, true and perfect hair dye. No ridiculous tints—no disappointment—harmless, reliable, instantaneous black or brown. At all druggists and No. 16 Bond St.
—*The New York Times*, 1873.

BURNETT'S KALLISTON

For the Complexion...Of all the compounds we have yet seen prepared as a cosmetic for the skin, there is none that has a higher reputation, or one that is so popular with the ladies, as the far-famed KALLISTON. It is scientifically prepared, and is a perfume as well as a toilet wash. It will, with a few applications, remove tan, freckles, sunburn, and all cutaneous eruptions. It is extensively used for these purposes, and ladies who apply it can experience no inconvenience from rough or irritated skin. Joseph Burnett & Co., are the Proprietors—Boston Transcript....for sale by dealers generally. Price 50 cents a bottle.
—*Harper's Weekly*, 1861.

BURNETT'S COCOAINE

Premature loss of the hair, which is so common now-a-days, may be entirely prevented by use of Burnett's Cocoaine. It has been used in thousands of cases where the hair was coming out in handfuls, and has never failed to arrest its decay, and to promote a healthy and vigorous growth. It is, at the same time, unrivaled as a dressing for the hair. A single application will render it soft and glossy for several days.

—*Harper's Weekly*, 1861.

COSMOLINE

Cosmoline and Cosmoline Pomade, 50 cents a bottle, E. F. Foughton, Philadelphia, Pa.

— The *Scranton* [Pa.] *Weekly Republican*, January 5, 1875.

BLOOM OF YOUTH

Secret of beauty. How to beautify the complexion. If there is one wish dearer than another to the heart of woman, it is the desire to be beautiful. The wonderful reputation of GEO. W. LAIRD'S "BLOOM OF YOUTH" is very justly deserved. For improving and beautifying the skin, it is undoubtedly the best toilet preparation in the world. It is composed of entirely harmless materials; and, while the immediate effects are to render the skin a beautiful creamy white, it will, after a few applications, make it soft, smooth, and beautifully clear, removing all blemishes and discolorations. This delightful toilet preparation has been severely tested by the Board of Health of New York City. Dr. Louis A. Sayres, after carefully examining the analysis made by the above board, pronounced GEO. W. LAIRD'S "BLOOM OF YOUTH" harmless, and entirely free from anything injurious to the health or skin. Beware of counterfeits. Ask your druggist for GEO. W. LAIRD'S "BLOOM OF YOUTH." The genuine has the United States revenue stamp engraved on the front label, and the name, G. W. Laird, blown in the glass on the back of every bottle. Sold by all druggists and fancy goods dealers.

— *Harper's Weekly*, 1873.

ARCADIAN PINK

Lundborgs' new perfume Arcadian Pink, the most beautiful and natural perfume of the age! Entirely original, and made by no other perfumer. Sold by druggists, etc.

— *Harper's Bazaar*, 1871.

LUNDBORG'S PERFUMES

Lundborg's Perfumes, Edenia, Marechal Niel Rose, Aline Violet, Boya Lily. Lundborg's Rhenish Cologne. These perfumes are for sale by almost all druggists and dealers in toilet articles, but if, for any reason, they cannot be so obtained, send for a price list to Ladd & Coffin, Proprietors and Manufacturers, 24 Barclay St., cor. Church St., New York.

— *The Youth's Companion*, 1888.

LYON'S KATHAIRON

What a figure! Ha! Ha! Ha! This is the greeting often received from their friends, by those becoming prematurely grey or bald. To avoid anything so unpleasant you have only to use Lyon's Kathairon, the most excellent and popular preparation for the hair ever made. Sold everywhere.

— *Harper's Weekly*, 1861.

FLORIDA WATER

Summer is coming! It will not be long before the thermometer will be in the nineties, and you will be running off to the mountains or the seashore. Do not start without a supply of the delightful perfume Murray & Lanman's Florida Water. It is a most refreshing lotion after exposure to the sun. It cools the skin and removes the smart of sunburn.

—*The Chautauqua* [N.Y.] *Assembly Herald*, June 1892.

SOZODONT

Gemmed with pearls. A mouth gemmed with pearls flashes radiance every time it opens. The contrast between the ruby of lovely lips and the pearly teeth they inclosed has winged the fancy of many a poet. Sozodont, fair ones, is the thing that most contributes to adorn the feminine mouth. It is pure, it is aromatic, it retains the natural color of teeth incrusted with yellow tartar. No gritty or other objectionable ingredient contaminates it. Its odor is balmy, and its purifying operation thorough.

—*The Weekly Inter Ocean*, 1885.

202 Toiletry bottle. Patent lip. Transparent, blue glass with thickened, plain-lip neck finish and with deeply beveled corners. Molded with an inscription on the body: "DE LA COUR'S / BALM OF THE / WHITE WATER LILLY / CAMDEN, N.J." Height, 5 7/16 inches; base, 1 7/8 × 1 5/16 inches. Capacity, about 3 ounces. Fort Union, 1870–90.

203 Toiletry bottle. Transparent, colorless glass with flanged-lip neck finish. Molded with the inscription "PAT / APPLIED / FOR" inside circular depression in the center of the square base. Height, 2 5/8 inches; base, 1 1/2 × 1 1/2 inches. Capacity, about 2 ounces. Fort Union, 1865–90.

202

203

204 Toiletry bottle. Fluted, prescription style. Transparent, blue glass with flanged-lip neck finish. Molded. Height, 3 1/8 inches; diameter of the 12-sided base, 1 3/4 inches. Capacity, about 4 ounces. Fort Union, 1865–90.

205 Toiletry bottle. Transparent, colorless glass with a flanged-lip neck finish. Molded with a petal design on the shoulder and another above the foot. Height, 5 inches; base, 1 7/8 × 1 1/4 inches. Capacity, about 3 ounces. Fort Union, 1865–90.

204

205

206

207

206 Toiletry bottle. Transparent, colorless glass with a thickened, plain-lip neck finish. Molded. The remnant of the paper label reads: "POMM(A).../P... L... / POUR LA TO...ETT... / E. COUD... / ___." Height, 3 7/8 inches; base, 2 × 1 1/4 inches. Capacity, about 4 ounces. Fort Union, 1865–90.

207 Toiletry bottle. Transparent, colorless glass with a flanged-lip neck finish. Molded. Height, 6 1/8 inches; base, 1 3/4 × 1 1/4 inches. Capacity, about 4 ounces. Fort Union, 1865–90.

208

209

208 Toiletry bottle, probably a bay rum dispenser. Taper shape, sprinkle-top, cologne style. Transparent, colorless glass with a narrow, rounded-collar neck finish. Molded in the center of the base is the number "551". Height, 7 5/8 inches; base diameter, 1 3/4 inches. Capacity, about 10 ounces. Fort Union, 1865–90.

209 Toiletry bottle. Transparent, colorless glass with a narrow, rounded-collar neck finish. Molded in the center of the base is the letter "W". Height, 4 3/8 inches; base diameter, 1 3/4 inches. Capacity, about 5 ounces. Fort Union, 1865–90.

210

211

210 Toiletry bottle. Transparent, colorless glass with three narrow rounded rings forming the neck finish. Molded. Centered in the concave base are the inscribed letters "W&S". Figure illustrates, in a duplicate specimen, the opposite side of the bottle. Height, 3 7/8 inches; base diameter, 1 3/8 inches. Capacity, about 2 ounces. Fort Union, 1865–90.

211 Toiletry bottle. Transparent, colorless glass with a thickened, plain-lip neck finish. Molded. Height, 3 inches; base diameter, 1 1/8 inches. Capacity, about 1 ounce. Fort Union, 1865–90.

212 Toiletry bottle. Transparent, colorless glass with a thickened, plain-lip neck finish. Molded. Height, 4 7/8 inches; base, 1 1/2 × 1 1/2 inches. Capacity, about 3 ounces. Fort Union, 1865–90.

213 Toiletry bottle. Transparent, colorless glass with a thickened, plain-lip neck finish. Molded with in situ label which appears to have been applied in reverse over another label. Label: "_____ / PIV... / PAR...". Height, 4 7/8 inches; base diameter, 1 1/4 inches. Capacity, about 3 ounces. Fort Union, 1865–90.

212

213

214 Toiletry bottle. Transparent, colorless glass with a flanged-lip neck finish. Molded. Height, 4 3/16 inches; base, 2 × 1 3/8 inches. Capacity, about 2 1/2 inches. Fort Union, 1865–90.

215 Toiletry bottle. Transparent, blue glass with a narrow, rounded-ring neck finish. Molded. Height, 7 1/8 inches; diameter of irregular base, about 1 3/4 inches. Capacity, about 7 ounces. Fort Union, 1865–90.

214

215

216 Toiletry bottle. Fluted prescription style. Transparent, colorless glass with a flanged-lip neck finish. Molded. Height, 5 1/4 inches; diameter of the 12-sided base, 1 3/4 inches. Capacity, about 6 ounces. Fort Union, 1865–90.

217 Toiletry bottle. Transparent, colorless glass with a thickened, plain-lip neck finish. Molded. Height, 4 3/4 inches; base, 2 1/8 × 7/8 inches. Capacity, about 3 ounces. Fort Union, 1865–90.

216

217

218

219

220

221

222

223

218 Toiletry bottle. Transparent, blue glass with a broad-collar neck finish. Molded. Inscribed in the round base is "Mᶜ C". Height, 4 3/4 inches; base diameter, 1 3/8 inches. Capacity, about 3 ounces. Fort Union, 1865–90.

219 Toiletry bottle. Paneled, flat oval style. Transparent, colorless glass with a flaring-lip neck finish. Molded, with "E B" near the perimeter of a circular basal depression. Height, 3 1/2 inches; base, 1 1/4 × 2 1/8 inches. Capacity, about 4 ounces. Fort Union, 1865–90.

220 Toiletry bottle. Transparent, colorless glass with a prescription-lip neck finish. Molded. Height, 3 3/4 inches; base, 1 1/8 × 1 15/16 inches. Capacity, about 1 ounce. Fort Union, 1865–90.

221 Toiletry bottle. Transparent, colorless glass with a prescription-lip neck finish. Molded. Height, 3 1/2 inches; base, 1 1/8 × 1 1/2 inches. Capacity, about 4 ounces. Fort Union, 1875–90.

222 Toiletry bottle. Transparent, blue glass with a flaring-lip neck finish. Molded. Height, 5 3/4 inches; diameter of the 12-sided base, 2 inches. Capacity, about 8 ounces. Fort Union, 1865–90.

223 Toiletry bottle. Transparent, blue glass with a double-ring neck finish. Three narrow rings decorate the cylindrical neck. Molded. Height, 8 inches; base diameter, 2 1/4 inches. Capacity, about 11 ounces. Fort Union, 1865–90.

224 Toiletry bottle. Transparent, blue glass with a double-ring neck finish. Molded. Height, 9 3/4 inches; base diameter, 2 1/4 inches. Capacity, about 11 ounces. Fort Union, 1865–90.

225 Toiletry bottle. Transparent, colorless glass with a flaring-lip neck finish. Well-executed molded imitation of cut glass. The base is marked with a molded rosette covering most of the surface. Height, 4 1/2 inches; base diameter, 2 inches. Capacity, about 6 ounces. Fort Union, 1875–90.

224

225

226 Toiletry bottle. Transparent, colorless glass with a thickened, plain-lip neck finish. Molded. Height, 5 3/8 inches; base diameter, 1 5/16 inches. Capacity, about 3 ounces. Fort Union, 1880–90.

227 Toiletry (?) bottle. Transparent, colorless glass with a flaring-lip neck finish. Molded with "484" in the base. Height, 2 1/8 inches; base, 1 ×1 1/2 inches. Capacity, about 2 ounces. Fort Union, 1865–85.

226

227

228 Toiletry (?) bottle. Transparent, colorless glass with a flaring-lip neck finish. Molded in a two-piece mold. Height, 5 1/4 inches; diameter of the 12-sided base, 1 7/8 inches. Capacity, about 5 ounces. Fort Union, 1865–75.

229 Toilet water bottle. Transparent, light-blue glass, with a broad, sloping-collar neck finish. Molded with an inscription on a cylindrical body: "FLORIDA WATER / MURRAY & LANMAN / DRUGGISTS / NEW YORK". The number "63" is molded in the center of a concave base. Height, 9 inches; base diameter, 2 1/8 inches. Capacity, about 9 ounces. Fort Union, 1870–90.

228

229

230

231

232

233

234

235

230 Toilet water (?) bottle. Transparent, blue glass with a broad, sloping-collar neck finish. Molded. Height, 5 7/8 inches; base diameter, 1 3/4 inches. Capacity, about 7 ounces. Fort Union, 1863–90.

231 Perfume bottle. Round, Lubin style. Transparent, colorless glass with a plain neck finish. Molded with an inscription on a cylindrical body: "COLGATE & CO / PERFUMERS / NEW YORK". Height, 3 1/8 inches; base diameter, 1 1/2 inches. Capacity, about 2 ounces. Fort Union, 1870–90.

232 Perfume bottle. Transparent, colorless glass with a flanged-lip neck finish. Molded with an inscription inside an oval enclosure on a cylindrical body: "F HOYT & CO / PERFUMERS / PHILAD'A". Height, 3 7/8 inches; base diameter, 1 1/4 inches. Capacity, about 2 ounces. Fort Union, 1870–90.

233 Perfume bottle. Transparent, colorless glass with a flanged-lip neck finish. Molded with an inscription on a cylindrical body: "LUBIN / PARFUMEUR / PARIS". Ground-glass stopper and contents in situ. Height, 3 1/8 inches; base diameter, 1 1/2 inches. Capacity, about 2 ounces. Fort Union, 1865–90.

234 Perfume bottle. Transparent, colorless glass with a flaring-lip neck finish. Molded with a vertical inscription on the body: "HARRISON'S / COLUMBIAN / PERFUMERY". Height, 2 7/8 inches; base, 1 1/2 × 1 1/2 inches. Capacity, about 3 ounces. Fort Union, 1865–90.

235 Perfume bottle. Transparent, colorless glass with a ring neck finish. Molded. Height, 3/4 inch; base, 1 × 1 inch. Capacity, about 1/2 ounce. Fort Union, 1870–90.

236 Perfume bottle. Transparent, green glass with a plain neck finish. Molded. Height, 2 3/8 inches; base, 1/2 × 7/16 inch. Capacity, about 1/4 ounce. Fort Union, 1880–90.

237 Perfume bottle. Short caswell style. Transparent, colorless glass with a thickened, plain-lip neck finish. Molded. Height, 2 5/8 inches; base diameter, 1 1/2 inches. Capacity, about 2 ounces. Fort Union, 1880–90.

236   237

238 Perfume (?) bottle. Transparent, colorless glass with a prescription-lip neck finish. Molded. Height, 2 inches; base, 7/8 × 1/2 inch. Capacity, about 1/2 ounce. Fort Union, 1863–90.

239 Perfume (?) bottle. Transparent, pale blue glass with a prescription-lip neck finish. Molded. Height, 1 5/8 inches; diameter of an octagonal base, 3/4 inch. Capacity, about 1/4 ounce. Fort Union, 1875–90.

238   239

240 Perfume bottle. Transparent, blue glass with a thickened, plain-lip neck finish. Molded with an inscription on a corner-fluted, rectangular body: "GENUINE / ESSENCE." Height, 4 7/16 inches; base, 1 3/16 × 11/16 inches. Capacity, about 1 1/2 ounces. Fort Laramie, 1870–90.

241 Perfume bottle. Round, Lubin style. Transparent, colorless glass with a flanged-lip neck finish and with a ground-glass stopper. Molded with an inscription on a cylindrical body: "ESS. BOUQUET / LUBIN." Height, 2 3/8 inches; base diameter 1 1/2 inches. Capacity, about 1 ounce. Fort Laramie, 1870–90.

240   241

242

243

244

245

246

247

242 Perfume bottle. Transparent, colorless glass with a ring-lip neck finish. Molded with an inscription on the body: "LUNDBORG / NEW YORK." Height, 1 15/16 inches; base diameter, 1 1/8 inches. Capacity, about 1/2 ounce. Fort Laramie, 1885–90.

243 Perfume bottle. Transparent, colorless glass with a thickened, plain-lip neck finish. Molded with an inscription on the body: "LUBIN / PARFUMEUR / PARIS". An identical specimen was recovered at Fort Union. Height, 3 1/8 inches; base diameter, 1 1/2 inches. Capacity, about 1 ounce. Fort Laramie, 1865–90.

244 Perfume (?) bottle. Transparent, colorless glass with a thickened, plain-lip neck finish. Molded. Height, 1 3/4 inches; base diameter, 15/16 inch. Capacity, about 1/2 ounce. Fort Laramie, 1880–90.

245 Perfume (?) bottle. Transparent, colorless glass with a thickened, plain-lip neck finish. Molded. Height, 2 3/8 inches; diameter of the octagonal base, 3/4 inch. Capacity, about 1/2 ounce. Fort Laramie, 1870–90.

246 Perfume (?) bottle. Transparent, colorless glass with a thickened, plain-lip neck finish. Molded. Height, 2 inches; base diameter, 1 inch. Capacity, about 1/2 ounce. Fort Laramie, 1885–90.

247 Perfume (?) bottle. Transparent, colorless glass with a thickened, plain-lip neck finish. Molded. Height, 2 1/2 inches; base diameter, 1 1/2 inches. Capacity, about 1 ounce. Fort Laramie, 1880–90.

248 Perfume (?) bottle. Transparent, colorless glass with a thickened, plain-lip neck finish. Molded. Height, 2 13/16 inches; base diameter, 13/16 inch. Capacity, about 1/2 ounce. Fort Laramie, 1880–90.

249 Perfume (?) bottle. Transparent, colorless glass with a thickened, plain-lip neck finish. Molded. Height. 1 5/8 inches; diameter of the octagonal base, 3/4 inch. Capacity, about 1/4 ounce. Fort Laramie, 1875–90.

248

249

250 Perfume (?) bottle. Transparent, colorless glass with a bead neck finish. Molded. Height, 3 1/8 inches; base, 1 11/16 × 1 7/16 inches. Capacity, about 1 ounce. Fort Laramie, 1875–90.

251 Cologne bottle. Transparent, colorless glass. Type of neck finish is unknown. Molded with a circular inscription on a rectangular body: "ED PINAUD / PARIS". A bowl of flowers is molded in relief above the inscription near the shoulder. Height, 5 3/8 inches; base, 1 3/8 × 1 7/8 inches. Capacity, about 7 ounces. Fort Union, 1870–90.

250

251

252 Cologne bottle. Transparent, colorless glass with a flanged-lip neck finish. Molded in the form of a male human effigy, probably representing Napoleon Bonaparte. Height, 7 1/4 inches; base diameter, 2 inches. Capacity, about 8 ounces. Fort Union, 1865–90.

253 Cologne (?) bottle. Transparent, colorless glass with a flanged-lip neck finish. Molded with an inscription on a cylindrical body: "X. BAZIN / PHILADᴬ". Height, 3 1/8 inches; base diameter, 1 3/4 inches. Capacity, about 3 ounces. Fort Union, 1850–69.

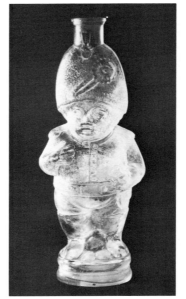

252

253

254

255

256

258

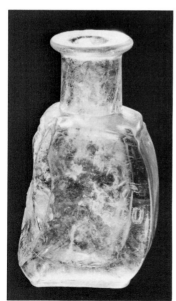

259

257

254 Cologne (?) bottle. Transparent, colorless glass with a flanged-lip neck finish. Molded with a horizontal inscription on a rectangular body: "HARRISON'S / COLUMBIAN / PERFUMERY." Height, 3 3/4 inches; base, 1 7/8 × 1 7/8 inches. Capacity, about 6 ounces. Fort Union, 1865–90.

255 Cologne bottle. Transparent, colorless glass with a prescription-lip neck finish. Molded with an inscription on a cylindrical body: "AUSTEN'S / FOREST FLOWER / CO-LOGNE / W. J. AUSTEN / & CO / OSWEGO N Y". Inscribed in the center of the concave base is the letter "D". According to the label this article was priced at 15 cents. Height, 3 1/16 inches; base diameter, 1 1/8 inches. Capacity, about 1/2 ounce. Fort Laramie, 1875–90.

256 Cologne bottle. Transparent, colorless glass with a bead neck finish. Molded with an inscription on the body: "KIRK & COMP^Y / (a circle) / CHICAGO." Remnant of the paper label reads: "ZENITHIA / COLOGNE / KI... & COMP^Y." Centered in the base is the numeral "8". Height, 3 1/4 inches; base diameter, 1 3/16 inches. Capacity, about 1 ounce. Fort Laramie, 1880–90.

257 Cologne bottle. Transparent, colorless glass with a thickened, plain-lip neck finish. Molded. The remnant of the paper label reads: "DOUBLE / ... AU / ———" Height, 6 3/16 inches; base, 2 3/16 × 1 3/16 inches. Capacity, about 5 ounces. Fort Laramie, 1875–90.

258 Cologne bottle. Transparent, colorless glass with a thickened, plain-lip neck finish. Molded. Height, 3 5/8 inches; base, 15/16 × 1 7/16 inches. Capacity, about 2 ounces. Fort Laramie, 1875–85.

259 Cologne (?) bottle. Transparent, colorless glass with a flaring neck finish. Molded with an inscription on the body: "(BU)LLOCK / (W)ARD & CO / CHICAGO". This bottle was made especially for Bullock and Ward, post traders at Fort Laramie. Height, 3 1/8 inches; base, 3/4 × 1 3/16 inches. Capacity, about 3 ounces. Fort Laramie, 1865–68.

260 Cologne (?) bottle. Transparent, colorless glass with a thickened plain-lip neck finish. Molded. Height, 3 13/16 inches; base, 2 1/16 × 2 1/16 inches. Capacity, about 5 ounces. Fort Laramie, 1880–90.

261 Cologne or perfume bottle with a cork stopper and metal finial. Transparent, colorless glass with a thickened, plain-lip neck finish above a narrow, rounded ring. Molded with a circular inscription on a rectangular body: "E. COUDRAY / A / PARIS". Height, 3 3/4 inches; base, 1 5/8 × 1 5/8 inches. Capacity, about 3 ounces. Fort Union, 1870–90.

260

261

262 Cologne or perfume bottle. Transparent, colorless glass with a neck finish that has a crudely flanged lip. Molded with an inscription on a flask-shaped body: "CHRISTIANI / de / PARIS". Height, 3 3/8 inches; base, 1 7/8 × 1 1/4 inches. Capacity, about 4 ounces. Fort Union, 1865–90.

263 Cologne or perfume bottle. Short, blake style. White, opaque glass with a flanged-lip neck finish. Molded with an inscription on a rectangular body: "G. W. LAIRD / PERFUMER / NEW YORK". Height, 4 5/8 inches; base, 2 1/4 × 1 1/4 inches. Capacity, about 4 ounces. Fort Union, 1870–90.

262

263

264 Cologne or perfume bottle. Transparent, colorless glass. Molded with broad fluted corners and with a flanged-lip neck finish. A narrow, rounded collar occurs about 3/4 inch below the lip. Height, 4 7/8 inches; base, 1 7/8 × 7/8 inches. Capacity, about 4 ounces. Fort Union, 1865–90.

265 Cologne or perfume bottle. Transparent, colorless glass. Type of neck finish is unknown. Molded with an inscription on a cylindrical body: "ED PINAUD / (a circle) / PARIS." A bowl of flowers is molded in relief immediately above this lettering. The circular base broken but inscribed "...AC...". Height, unknown; base diameter, 1 3/8 inches. Capacity, about 3 ounces. Fort Union, 1865–90.

264

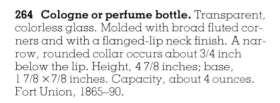

265

266

267

266 Cologne or perfume bottle. Transparent, colorless glass with a thickened, plain-lip neck finish. Molded. Height, 2 1/2 inches; diameter of the 12-sided base, 1 1/2 inches. Capacity, about 2 ounces. Fort Union, 1865–85.

267 Cologne or perfume bottle. Transparent, colorless glass with a flaring-lip neck finish. Molded with an inscription on a cylindrical body: "X. BAZIN / PERFUMEUR / PHILADEL-PHIA." Height, 3 9/16 inches; base diameter, 2 inches. Capacity, about 4 ounces. Fort Laramie, 1850–69.

268

268 Lotion bottle. Transparent, colorless glass with a thickened, plain-lip neck finish. Molded with an inscription on a rectangular body: "ESPEY'S / TRADE (figure) MARK / CREAM / FRAGRANT / . . . st Best And Most D(B?). . .tiful / . . .on in the WORLD for chapped hands. /_____ and ROUGHNESS of the Skin. /_____ Perfect Subst. . .e For C. . .erine, / . . .MPH. . .R ICE, COLD . . .EARM. . .C. / WITH-OUT BEING STICK. . . GREASY / KID GLOVE . . . / . . .E WORM IMMEDIATELY AFTER USING. / . . .es the Skin beautifully Soft, White & Smooth. / *(REM)*OVES SUNBURN AND TAN. / GEN^{L}: DEPOT NEW YORK." Height, 4 5/8 inches; base, 1 5/8 × 1 1/16 inches. Capacity, about 2 ounces. Fort Union, 1870–90.

269

270

269 Cologne or perfume bottle. Transparent, colorless glass with a thickened, plain-lip neck finish. Molded. Height, 4 inches; base, 1 9/16 × 1 1/8 inches. Capacity, about 2 ounces. Fort Laramie, 1875–90.

270 Bay rum bottle. Transparent, blue glass with a broad, rounded-collar neck finish. Molded with the remnant of the original label in situ indicating contents. Height, 7 3/4 inches; base diameter, 2 inches. Capacity, about 8 ounces. Fort Union, 1865–90.

271 Bay rum bottle. Transparent, colorless glass with thickened plain-lip neck finish. Molded. Remnant of the paper label reads: "FINE / BAY RUM / _____ / _____ / ...MICAL WORKS / TRADE MARK / TRADE MARK / TRADE MARK / TRADE MARK / _____ / _____ / _____ / CHIC...." Height, 5 1/4 inches; base, 1 1/2 × 1 1/4 inches. Capacity, about 3 ounces. Fort Laramie, 1875–90.

272 Complexion treatment bottle. Opaque white glass with a bead neck finish. Molded with an inscription on a rectangular body: "HAGAN'S MAGNOLIA / BALM." Height, 5 1/16 inches; base, 2 1/16 × 1 1/2 inches. Capacity, about 5 ounces. Fort Laramie, 1870–90.

271   272

273 Hair-preparation bottle. Ginger panel style. Transparent, light-blue or light-green glass with a rounded-collar neck finish above a narrow ring. Molded with an inscription on a rectangular body: "LYONS / KATHAIRON / FOR THE HAIR / NEW YORK." This inscription sometimes reads: "KATHAIRON / LYON'S / NEW YORK / FOR THE HAIR." Height, 6 1/2 inches; base, 1 1/4 × 1 7/8 inches. Capacity, about 4 ounces. Fort Union, 1860–90.

274 Hair-preparation bottle. Transparent, blue glass with a beveled-ring neck finish. Molded with an inscription near the perimeter of the base: "WALKER'S / V. B." Paper label text: "W..." In the center of the base is the underlined numeral "7". Height, 8 1/4 inches; base diameter, 3 1/8 inches. Capacity, about 22 ounces. Fort Laramie, 1885–90.

273   274

275 Hair-preparation bottle. Transparent, blue glass with a broad, sloping-collar neck finish. Molded with an inscription on the body: "PARKER'S / HAIR / BALSAM / NEW YORK." Height, 8 inches; base, 2 7/8 × 1 3/4 inches. Capacity, about 9 ounces. Fort Laramie, 1880–90.

276 Hair-dressing bottle. Transparent, colorless glass with a flanged-lip neck finish. Molded with an inscription on a rectangular body: "AMOLE / HAIR / DRESSING / (ALCo monogram inside a small circle) / (a leaf) / AZTEC / LABORATORY / COMPANY / MANUFACTURERS / SANTA FE / N. M." Height, 5 inches; base, 2 × 3/8 inches. Capacity, about 6 ounces. Fort Union, 1865–90.

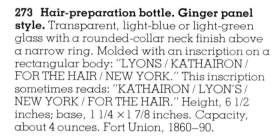

275   276

277

278

277 Hair-dressing bottle. Transparent, color-less glass with a thickened, plain-lip neck finish. Molded with an inscription on the body: "A. J. WALKER / CoCo / HAIR DRESSER / DRUGGIST". Height, 6 1/2 inches; base, 2 1/4 × 1 1/4 inches. Capacity, about 5 ounces. Fort Laramie, 1880–90.

278 Hair-oil bottle. Transparent, colorless glass with a flanged-lip neck finish. Molded with an hexagonal base and a fluted body. An adhering remnant of a paper label reads: "ROSE BUD HAIR OIL STANDARD PERFUM-ERY Co. NEW YORK". Inscribed in the center of the concave base are the letters "W & S". Height, 6 inches; base diameter, 1 3/4 inches. Capacity, about 4 ounces. Fort Union, 1865–90.

279

280

279 Hair-oil bottle. Transparent, colorless glass with a thickened plain-lip neck finish. Molded. Height, 5 13/16 inches; base, 1 ×2 3/4 inches. Capacity, about 5 ounces. Fort Laramie, 1880–90.

280 Hair-oil (?) bottle. Transparent, colorless glass with a thickened plain-lip neck finish. Molded. Height, 5 9/16 inches; base, 7/8 ×2 3/8 inches. Capacity, about 3 ounces. Fort Laramie, 1870–90.

281

282

281 Hair-dye bottle. Transparent, light-green glass. Molded with an inscription on a rectan-gular body: "BATCHELOR'S / LIQUID / HAIR DYE / N⁰ 1." Height, 3 1/8 inches; base, 1 1/4 × 1 1/4 inches. Capacity, about 2 ounces. Fort Laramie, 1850–90.

282 Scalp-treatment bottle. Transparent, light-blue glass with a prescription-lip neck finish. Molded with an inscription on a rec-tangular body: "BURNETT / BURNETT'S / COCOAINE / BOSTON." Height, 7 1/8 inches; base, 2 1/2 ×1 1/2 inches. Capacity, about 9 ounces. Fort Union, 1860–90.

283 Scalp-treatment bottle. Transparent, pale green glass with a thickened, plain-lip neck finish. The remnant of the paper label begins: "...lls vegeta... / _____ hair _____", after which there are some 25 lines, mostly illegible. Near the bottom of the label is: "_____ genuine unless signed _____ Proprietors. _____ / REUBEN P. HALL (script) / _____ Congress in the year 1866 by R.P. Hall & Co. in the Clerks Office _____ the D... / ...ording to act of Congress 1870, in the office of the chairman of Congres(s) at Washington _____." Molded with the letter "H" near the center of the base. Height, 6 9/16 inches; base 2 7/8 × 1 9/16 inches. Capacity, about 8 ounces. Fort Laramie, 1866–90.

284 Dandruff-cure (?) bottle. Transparent, colorless glass with a thickened plain-lip neck finish. Molded. Height, 5 7/8 inches; base, 1 1/8 ×3 inches. Capacity, about 5 ounces. Fort Laramie, 1885–90.

283   284

285 Pomade jar. Transparent, colorless glass with a narrow, rounded-collar neck finish. Molded with an inscription on a cylindrical body: "REGISTERED / COSMOLINE (superimposed upon a globe with latitude and longitude lines) / TRADE MARK". The letter "D" is inscribed in the center of its concave base. Height, 2 7/8 inches; base diameter, 2 inches. Capacity, about 5 ounces. Fort Union, 1865–90.

286 Pomade jar. Translucent, white glass. Molded bear effigy in two pieces with the head forming the cap of the jar. Height, with the head attached, 4 1/2 inches, and without the head attached, 3 1/4 inches; base, 2 1/4 × 1 3/8 inches. Capacity, about 3 ounces. Fort Union, 1865–90.

285   286

287 Dentifrice bottle. Metal, sprinkler top. Transparent, colorless glass with a thickened, plain-lip neck finish. Molded with an inscription on a rectangular body: "VAN BUSKIRK'S / FRAGRANT / SOZODONT". This bottle is probably an earlier version of No. 288. Height, 5 5/8 inches; base, 1 × 1 15/16 inches. Capacity, about 3 ounces. Fort Union, 1865–90.

288 Dentifrice bottle. Transparent, colorless glass with flanged-lip neck finish. Molded with an inscription on a rectangular body: "FRAGRANT SOZODONT / FOR THE TEETH,/ AND BREATH / VAN BUSKIRK'S". Height, 6 1/4 inches; base, 2 × 1 1/8 inches. Capacity, about 3 ounces. Fort Laramie, 1870–1900.

287   288

Household products such as bluing and blacking compounds were packaged in bottles long before the late nineteenth century. This was not true of most food products, however, which, like beer, awaited development of pasteurization before substantial activity in production and distribution could take place. Exceptions to this were stable foods, i.e., those with a high sugar content, such as jellies; those having high acidity, such as pepper sauce, mustards, and pickles; and extracts which required the addition of alcohol in their preparation. Such foods were commonly packaged in glass and were standard items of commercial distribution by the last half of the nineteenth century.

Considering these conditions, it is quite significant that certain bottles were *not* found. Conspicuously absent from the collections are jars for jams, jellies, honey, molasses, and oils. Pickle, mustard, and relish jars are rare. All such products were packaged in glass and were in common supply as items of commercial trade by the late nineteenth century. It can be concluded that such products were standard items stocked in bulk by the army commissary and that their purchase in small containers was unnecessary. Certain products, such as pickles and molasses, are known to have been standard commissary items because of their antiscorbutic properties. However, too great a reliance should not be placed on this explanation in the case of jellies, mustards, or honey, and the near total absence of jars for these products is difficult to explain.

The absence of Mason fruit jars is also significant. During the time the forts were occupied, these jars were in widespread use for the home preserving of fruits, vegetables, and meats. Since they were not found, it must be assumed that army households did little preserving for their own use and appear to have relied entirely upon the army commissary or the sutler for their needs. This difference from their civilian counterparts may be explained in part by the peripatetic nature of army life, which made stockpiling foodstuffs preserved in fragile containers impractical. Another contributing factor may have involved the difficulty of obtaining fresh foods in the West. Gardens did not grow easily or well in this semi-arid land, and even the most diligent person could seldom produce a summer garden capable of providing a surplus to immediate family needs.

The only bottles found approaching the use and form of fruit jars are two which resemble early pre-Mason jars, i.e., a type called an English pickle bottle. These bottles contained prepared baby foods and constitute a most interesting bit of historical evidence. While we have no way of knowing their specific contents, these jars present clear and certain evidence of the emerging revolution in the food industry—commercially produced and packaged perishable foods. Whether they contained meat, milk, fruits, or vegetables, we may be certain that baby food then was not likely to have been highly acidic, alcoholic, or sufficiently sweetened to insure preservation. These jars can only testify to the use of pasteurization in a dependable, air tight container. They must have seemed a godsend to army mothers who, until then, had been forced to sustain their infants on cereals, dried fruits, dubious meats, and an occasional durable vegetable such as potatoes or onions.

Other bottles doubtless represent culinary indulgences purchased at the sutler's store. It is not surprising that many extract bottles were found, for army ladies and laundresses were frequent bakers. The presence of pepper-sauce bottles, too, is quite in harmony with the conditions of army life. Meat was supplied by civilians to the Commissary Department under terms of sharply drawn contracts. Delivered to a post on the hoof, it was butchered directly. When one considers the truly primitive sanitary conditions at most posts and the almost total absence of cooling facilities for foods, it is easy to understand why army families, and perhaps even enlisted men, apparently spent large sums of hard-earned money on pepper sauces.

The specimens described below are those which are known to have contained food, or a product associated with the preparation of food. Products of characteristically domestic use, such as laundry bluing, are also included, as well as bottles for miscellaneous products which seemed to fit precisely into none of the other categories.

LEA & PERRIN'S WORCESTERSHIRE SAUCE

Citizens called from their homes on public duty and deprived of many personal comforts, need not be deprived of Lea & Perrin's Worcestershire Sauce, as the use of this esteemed condiment will go far to remedy the discomforts arising from bad or irregular cooking. For sale in half-pint, pint, and quart bottles, by all respectable grocers, throughout the United States. John Duncan & Sons, Union Square and 14th Street, Sole Agents.

—*Harper's Weekly*, 1861.

MELLIN'S FOOD

Mellin's Food for infants and invalids. The only perfect substitute for mother's milk. The most nourishing diet for invalids and nursing mothers. Commended by all physicians. Keeps in all climates. Sold by all druggists. 75¢. Send for pamphlet. T. Metcalf & Co., 41 Central Wharf, Boston, Mass.

—*The Saint Paul and Minneapolis Pioneer Press*, 1883.

DR. PRICE'S SPECIAL FLAVORING EXTRACTS

Natural fruit flavors. Dr. Price's Special Flavoring Extracts. Prepared from the choicest fruits, without coloring, poisonous oils, acids, or artificial essences. Always uniform in strength, without any adulterations or impurities. Have gained their reputation from their perfect purity, superior strength and quality. Admitted by all who have used them as the most delicate, grateful and natural flavors for cakes, puddings, creams, etc. ever made. Manufactured by Steele & Price, makers of Lupulin Yeast Gems, Cream Baking Powder, etc., Chicago and St. Louis.

—*The Chicago Daily Tribune*, 1882.

SPALDING'S GLUE

Money may be tight, but it is nothing to SPALDING'S GLUE. That's the tightest thing out.

—*The Times-Democrat*, New Orleans, 1883.

VAN STAN'S STRATENA

Van Stan's Stratena the very best cement in the world. Invaluable also for mending glass, wood, china, jewelry, ornaments, and all light metals. Perfectly transparent. The only cement given a space at the Centennial. None genuine but has blown in the bottles 'VAN STAN'S STRATENA.' All others are base frauds. For sale by druggists and other dealers. Sample bottles sent by mail, postage paid, on receipt of thirty cents in postage stamps or money, by Van Stan's Stratena Co. (limited), 287 So. Third St., Phil., successors to Kennan & Co., sole manufacturers and owners of trade mark and right to manufacture in the United States

—*The Youth's Companion*, Boston, May 9, 1878.

289 Culinary bottle. Transparent, blue glass with basal fluting. Flaring neck finish with a narrow ring beneath. Blown mold. The base is scarred with a pontil mark. Height, 9 13/16 inches; base diameter, 2 1/2 inches. Capacity, about 18 ounces. Fort Union, 1851–65.

290 Culinary (?) bottle. Transparent, colorless glass with a thickened, plain-lip neck finish. Molded with an inscription on the body: "H.F.A. PINCKNEY. & CO / LONDON." Height, 5 inches; base, 1 1/2 × 1 1/2 inches. Capacity, about 4 ounces. Fort Union, 1865–90.

289   **290**

291 Culinary (?) bottle. Transparent, blue glass with a prescription-lip neck finish. Molded. Height, 2 7/8 inches; base, 9/16 × 1 3/16 inches. Capacity, about 4 ounces. Fort Union, 1865–90.

292 Sauce bottle. Ginger panel with a double ring lip. Transparent, light-blue glass. The neck finish has a double rounded collar. Molded with an inscription on a rectangular body is "E. R. DURKEE & Cº / NEW YORK". Height, 4 1/2 inches; base, 1 5/8 × 7/8 inches. Capacity, about 1 ounce. Fort Union 1880–85.

291

292

293 Sauce bottle. Transparent, light-green glass with a broad-collar neck finish, with a narrow ring at the lip, and with another narrow ring below the collar. Molded cylindrical body and a round base. Inscription on the shoulder reads: "WORCESTERSHIRE SAUCE". Inscribed on the body: "LEA & PERRINS". Concave base bears the inscription "J / D / 10 (in the center) / S." The glass part of the glass/cork stopper found in situ is also inscribed "LEA & PERRINS". Height, 8 5/8 inches; base diameter, 2 1/2 inches. Capacity, about 13 ounces. Fort Union, 1851–90.

294 Sauce bottle. This specimen is almost identical to No. 293 except for its smaller size and its base, which is inscribed with letters in each of the four quadrants: "A / C / C (or B) / Co." Height, 7 1/8 inches; base diameter, 2 inches. Capacity, about 8 ounces. Fort Union, 1851–90.

293

294

295 Sauce bottle. Transparent, colorless glass with a thickened, plain-lip neck finish. Molded with an inscription on the narrow sides of the rectangular body: "BURNETT / BOSTON". The remnant of the paper label reads: "_____ F...ING IC... / ...LIES (M?)US-TARDS. SAU(CE?) / prepared by / JOSEPH BURNETT & _____ / BOSTON / DIRECTIONS / A _____ teaspoon _____ mo... / quart (ac?)cordi(ng?) _____ ..e taste." Height, 4 3/16 inches; base, 1 11/16 × 1 1/16 inches. Capacity, about 3 ounces. Fort Union, 1860–90.

296 Sauce (?) bottle. Transparent, blue glass with a broad, sloping-collar neck finish. Molded. Height, 6 1/2 inches; base, 1 × 2 inches. Capacity, about 6 ounces. Fort Union, 1865–90.

295

296

297

298

297 Sauce bottle. Transparent, light-blue glass with a thickened, plain-lip neck finish. Blown mold with an inscription on its flask-shaped body: "E. R. DURKEE & Co / NEW YORK." A pontil mark is centered in the oval base. This specimen was recovered in excavations of the New Bakery at Fort Laramie and undoubtedly represents one of the earliest bottles used by the Durkee Company. Height, 4 3/4 inches; base, 1 9/16 × 7/8 inches. Capacity, about 2 ounces. Fort Laramie, 1857–60.

298 Sauce (?) bottle. Transparent, colorless glass, with the neck finish unknown. Molded with an inscription on a rectangular body: "BOSTON/ (perched owl) / W H & Co / CHICAGO." Height, unknown; square base, 1 5/8 × 1 5/8 inches. Capacity, about 2 ounces. Fort Laramie, 1875–90.

299

300

299 Sauce (?) bottle. Transparent, green glass with a broad-collar neck finish, with a narrow ring at the lip and with another narrow ring below the collar. Height, 4 1/8 inches; base diameter, 1 1/2 inches. Capacity, about 2 ounces. Fort Laramie, 1880–90.

300 Sauce (?) bottle. Transparent, blue glass with a thickened plain-lip neck finish. Two small raised dots appear near the center of the base. Height, 5 5/16 inches; base diameter, 3 inches. Capacity, about 13 ounces. Fort Laramie, 1880–90.

301

302

301 Extract bottle. Ginger panel style. Transparent, blue glass with a thickened, plain-lip neck finish. Molded with an inscription on a rectangular body: "H. T. HELMBOLD / GENUINE / FLUID EXTRACTS / PHILADEL-PHIA". Height, 6 1/8 inches; base, 2 × 1 1/4 inches. Capacity, about 6 ounces. Fort Union, 1865–90.

302 Extract bottle. Oval panel style. Transparent, light-blue glass with a flanged-lip neck finish. Molded with an inscription on a rectangular body: "DR. PRICE'S / DELICIOUS / FLAVORING EXTRACTS". Height, 5 3/8 inches; base, 1 13/16 × 7/8 inches. Capacity, about 4 ounces. Fort Union, 1865–90.

303 Extract (?) bottle. Flat with side panels. Transparent, colorless glass with a thickened-lip neck finish. Molded with an inscription on a rectangular body: "BURNETT / BOSTON." The letter "B" is inscribed in the center of the base. Height, 4 5/16 inches; base, 1 3/4 × 1 1/8 inches. Capacity, about 2 ounces. Fort Union, 1865–90.

304 Extract (?) bottle. Tall blake. Transparent, green glass with a broad, sloping-collar neck finish above a narrow ring. The corners of the body are sharply beveled. Molded with an inscription on a rectangular body: " C & B." Height, 7 1/2 inches; base, 2 1/4 × 1 5/8 inches. Capacity, about 6 ounces. Fort Union, 1865–90.

303

304

305 Extract (?) bottle. Round shoulder, panel style. Transparent, colorless glass with a flanged-lip neck finish. Rectangular body and base. Molded with an inscription on the shoulder: "F. B. S." Height, 4 5/8 inches; base, 1 5/8 × 1 1/4 inches. Capacity, about 3 ounces. Fort Union, 1865–90.

306 Extract (?) bottle. Drug oval style. Transparent, blue glass with a thickened, plain-lip (?) neck finish. Molded with an inscription near the base of the flask-shaped body: "BOSTON / J. PRESTON." A pontil mark is centered in the oval base. Height, unknown; base, 1 1/2 × 13/16 inches. Capacity, about 5 ounces. Fort Union, 1860–65.

305

306

307 Extract bottle. Transparent, colorless glass with a thickened, plain-lip neck finish. Molded with an inscription on a rectangular body: "SELECT / FLAVORS." Shoulder inscribed "COLTON'S". Height, 4 15/16 inches; base, 1 × 1 3/4 inches. Capacity, about 2 ounces. Fort Laramie, 1880–90.

308 Extract bottle. Transparent, blue glass with a thickened, plain-lip neck finish. Molded with an inscription on a rectangular body: "MARTIN & / GOVERNMENT / FLAVORING EXTRACTS / OMAHA / KENNARD." Imperfectly molded in the center of the base is "M^c...". Height, 5 3/4 inches, base, 2 1/4 × 1 1/4 inches. Capacity, about 4 ounces. Fort Laramie, 1880–90.

307

308

309

310

311

312

313

314

309 Extract bottle. Transparent, colorless glass with a thickened, plain-lip neck finish. The remnant of the paper label reads: "4 OUNCES / W (inscribed within a horizontal, diamond-shaped enclosure) / B...AN... / PURE EXTRACT OF / LEMON / FOR FLAVORING / CA...S, / I...AM, / P...NOS, / PASTRY / ETC. / P...K...D FOR / _____ MURPHY / _____(?)_____ ...B. / MA...WITH / ...CH." Height, 6 1/2 inches; base, 2 1/4 × 1 1/8 inches. Capacity, about 4 ounces. Fort Laramie, 1875–90.

310 Extract (?) bottle. Transparent, blue glass with a thickened plain-lip neck finish. Molded with an inscription on a rectangular body: "BURNETT / BOSTON." The corners of the body are sharply beveled, nearly one-third the width of the base. Height, 5 5/8 inches; base, 2 3/8 × 1 1/4 inches. Capacity, about 4 ounces. Fort Laramie, 1870–90.

311 Extract (?) bottle. Transparent, blue glass with a thickened, plain-lip neck finish. Height, 2 1/16 inches; base diameter, 1 1/4 inches. Capacity, about 1 ounce. Fort Laramie, 1875–90.

312 Condiment bottle. Transparent, green glass with a thickened, plain-lip neck finish. Molded with an inscription on a sloping body: "SMITH & VANDERBEEK / NEW YORK & CHICAGO." Height, 11 1/16 inches; base diameter, 2 5/8 inches. Capacity, about 30 ounces. Fort Laramie, 1870–90.

313 Condiment bottle. Transparent, colorless glass with a thickened, plain-lip neck finish. Height, 3 3/16 inches; base diameter, 1 5/8 inches. Capacity, about 3 ounces. Fort Laramie, 1865–90.

314 Condiment bottle. Transparent, colorless glass with a thickened, plain-lip neck finish. Height, 4 7/8 inches; base diameter, 2 1/2 inches. Capacity, about 9 ounces. Fort Laramie, 1880–90.

315 Condiment bottle. Cathedral style.
Transparent, green glass with a sauce neck
finish. Height, 8 3/8 inches; base, 2 × 2 inches.
Capacity, about 7 ounces. Fort Laramie,
1850–90.

316 Condiment bottle. Transparent, pale
green glass with a thickened, plain-lip neck
finish. Molded with a shallow, round depression in the base, within a diamond-shaped
enclosure: "H R (within a square) Z (lopsided) /
7 (backwards)." Height, 7 5/8 inches; base,
2 5/8 × 2 5/8 inches. Capacity, about 20
ounces. Fort Laramie, 1865–90.

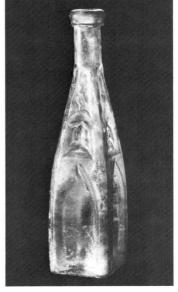 

315   316

317 Condiment (?) bottle. Transparent, pale
green glass with a thickened, plain-lip neck
finish. Height, 7 13/16 inches; base diameter,
2 15/16 inches. Capacity, about 24 ounces.
Fort Laramie, 1875–90.

318 Mustard jar. Transparent, colorless glass
with a thickened-lip neck finish. Molded with
an inscription on a cylindrical body:
"GULDEN'S." Inscribed around the perimeter
of the concave base: "PAT... / 8...". Height,
3 3/4 inches; base diameter, 2 1/2 inches.
Capacity, about 8 ounces. Fort Union, 1862–90.

317   318

319 Mustard jar. Transparent, colorless glass
with a plain neck finish. Molded with an inscription on the body: "F. B. STROUSE / NEW
YORK". Height, 2 5/8 inches; base diameter,
1 1/2 inches. Capacity, about 1 1/2 ounces.
Fort Union, 1870–90.

320 Mustard jar. Transparent, pale blue
glass. Ovoid in cross section. Plain-lip neck
finish with a wide ring beneath. Molded.
Height, 4 3/4 inches; base, 1 13/16 × 2 1/16
inches. Capacity, about 4 ounces. Fort Union,
1865–90.

319   320

321

322

323

324

325

326

321 Mustard jar. Transparent, colorless glass with a plain-rim neck finish. Molded. Height, 3 11/16 inches; base diameter, 1 15/16 inches. Capacity, about 5 ounces. Fort Union, 1851–61.

322 Chow chow jar. Transparent, green glass with a broad, thickened, plain-lip neck finish. Molded. The remnant of the paper label reads: "CHOW CHOW / CROSSE & BLACKWELL / BY APPOINTMENT / ESTA... / _____ / P...". Height, 8 1/8 inches; base, 4 1/16 inches. Capacity, about 38 ounces. Fort Laramie, 1875–90.

323 Pickle bottle. Gothic, or "cathedral," style. Transparent, blue glass with a crude, ring-lip neck finish and with a broad ring beneath. Molded. Height, 9 5/16 inches; base, 3 × 3 inches. Capacity, about 15 ounces. Fort Union, 1851–61.

324 Pickle (?) bottle. Transparent, colorless glass with an extract-lip neck finish. Molded. Height, 7 1/16 inches; base, 1 5/8 × 2 1/4 inches. Capacity, about 11 ounces. Fort Union, 1865–90.

325 Pickle or preserve bottle. Flat, caper style. Transparent, green glass with a thickened, plain-lip neck finish. Molded. Height, 8 7/8 inches; base, 1 3/4 × 1 1/8 inches. Capacity, about 5 ounces. Fort Union, 1880–85.

326 Pickle or preserve bottle. Transparent, pale green glass with a thickened, plain-lip neck finish. Molded. Height, 8 3/4 inches; base, 2 1/2 × 2 1/2 inches. Capacity, about 17 ounces. Fort Laramie, 1875–90.

327 Olive-oil bottle. Transparent, colorless glass with a thickened, plain-lip neck finish. Molded. Height, 9 7/8 inches; base diameter, 2 3/8 inches. Capacity, about 11 ounces. Fort Laramie, 1880–90.

328 Olive-oil bottle. Transparent, pale green glass with a thickened, plain-lip neck finish. Molded. The base has a kick-up similar to that of a wine bottle. Height, 12 3/4 inches; base diameter, 2 11/16 inches. Capacity, about 20 ounces. Fort Laramie, 1865–90.

327

328

329 Salad- or olive-oil bottle. Opaque green glass with a sauce neck finish. The remnant of the paper label reads: "...S... / S...LA... _____ / P...M... / _____ / PROV... / 107, 10..., / LEADEN *(HAL)* L ST / LONDON / AND AT...D... / ABERDEE *(N)* _____." Molded near perimeter of base: "298". Height, 12 1/4 inches; base diameter, 2 1/4 inches. Capacity, about 12 ounces. Fort Union, 1880–90.

330 Salad-dressing bottle. Transparent, blue glass with a flaring-lip neck finish. Molded. Recovered from a cellar at the site of the first Fort Union (1851–61), this bottle was made for the Durkee Company. Height, 7 5/8 inches; base, 2 1/2 ×2 1/2 inches. Capacity, about 12 ounces. Fort Union, 1857.

329

330

331 Baking-powder jar. Transparent, colorless glass with a rounded-collar neck finish. Molded with an inscription on the shoulder of a cylindrical body: "EDDY'S RELIABLE BAKING POWDER." Height, 4 7/8 inches; base diameter, 3 inches. Capacity, unknown. Fort Union, 1865–90.

332 Pepper-sauce bottle. Square (gothic) sauce style. Transparent, colorless glass with a narrow, rounded-collar neck finish. Height, 7 3/8 inches; base, 1 5/8 ×1 5/8 inches. Capacity, about 6 ounces. Fort Union, 1865–90.

331

332

333

334

335

336

337

338

333 Malted-milk bottle. Transparent, colorless glass with a continuous-thread neck finish. Molded with an inscription on a cylindrical body: "HORLICK'S / MALTED MILK". Centered in the concave base is the letter "b". Height, 3 5/16 inches; base diameter, 1 5/8 inches. Capacity, about 3 ounces. Fort Laramie, 1875–90.

334 Baby-food bottle. Old-style fruit bottle. Transparent, blue glass with a broad, sloping, rounded-collar neck finish. Molded with an inscription on the shoulder and cylindrical body: "SMALL SIZE / MELLIN'S / INFANT'S FOOD / DOLIBER GOODALE & Co / BOSTON". Height, 5 1/4 inches; base diameter, 3 1/2 inches. Capacity, about 6 ounces. Fort Union, 1865–90.

335 Baby-food bottle. Old-style fruit bottle. Transparent, blue glass with broad, plain, rounded-collar neck finish. Molded with an inscription on a cylindrical body: "MELLINS / INFANTS FOOD / T METCALF & CO / BOSTON". Height, 5 3/8 inches; base diameter, 2 5/8 inches. Capacity, about 10 ounces. Fort Union, 1865–90.

336 Nursing (?) bottle. Transparent, colorless glass with a narrow-ring neck finish. Molded. Height, 7 3/16 inches; base, 3 3/8 × 2 1/4 inches. Capacity, about 15 ounces. Fort Laramie, 1875–90.

337 Bluing bottle. Drug, oval style. Transparent, blue glass with a broad-collar neck finish. Molded with an inscription on its flask-shaped body: "BLUE / DOUBLE STRENGTH." Height, 6 inches; oval base, 2 1/4 × 1 1/4 inches. Capacity, about 6 ounces. Fort Union, 1865–90.

338 Bluing bottle. Plain, oval style. Transparent, blue glass with a broad-collar neck finish. Molded with an inscription on its flask-shaped body: "HUSBANDS / LAUNDRY / BLUE / DOUBLE STRENGTH." Height, 4 1/2 inches; oval base, 2 7/8 × 1 3/8 inches. Capacity, about 1 1/2 ounces. Fort Union, 1865–90.

339 Bluing (?) bottle. Transparent, blue glass with a broad-collar neck finish and with a narrow ring beneath. Height, 6 3/4 inches; base, 2 7/16 × 1 5/8 inches. Capacity, about 7 ounces. Fort Laramie, 1870–90.

340 Dye bottle. Transparent, blue glass with a broad-collar neck finish and with a narrow ring beneath. Molded with an inscription on its flask-shaped body: "HOWE / & / STEVENS / FAMILY / DYE COLORS." Height, 2 3/4 inches; base, 1 11/16 × 15/16 inches. Capacity, about 1 ounce. Fort Laramie, 1870–90.

339

340

341 Glue bottle. Wide mouth, prescription style. Transparent, blue glass with a thickened, plain-lip neck finish. Molded with an inscription on a cylindrical body: "SPALDING'S / GLUE". A pontil mark is centered in the concave base. Height, 3 1/4 inches; base diameter, 1 1/2 inches. Capacity, about 3 ounces. Fort Union, 1858–65.

342 Glue bottle. Transparent, colorless glass with a thickened, plain-lip neck finish. Molded with an inscription on a cylindrical body: "GOV'T. MUCILAGE / PATᴰ 1872." Height, 1 7/8 inches; base diameter, 2 9/16 inches. Capacity, about 2 ounces. Fort Laramie, 1872–90.

341

342

343 Glue bottle. Transparent, blue glass with a thickened, plain-lip neck finish. Molded with an inscription on a cylindrical body: "SPALDING'S / GLUE." Height, 3 3/16 inches; base diameter, 1 9/16 inches. Capacity, about 2 ounces. Fort Laramie, 1870–90.

344 Glue bottle. Transparent, blue glass with a plain neck finish. The small remnant of the paper label reads: " . . . AY(?) / _____ GL. . . / _____." Height, 3 5/16 inches; base diameter, 2 1/4 inches. Capacity, about 2 ounces. Fort Laramie, 1880–90.

343

344

345   **346**

347   **348**

349   **350**

345 Glue bottle. Transparent, blue glass with a ring-lip neck finish. The remnant of the paper label reads: "EXTRA / Adh... *(M?)*uci-lage, P... _____ By / _____ ...T, / _____." Height, 3 1/8 inches; diameter of the octagonal base, 2 5/8 inches. Capacity, about 2 ounces. Fort Laramie, 1880–90.

346 Glue bottle. Transparent blue glass with a ring-lip neck finish. Height, 3 1/16 inches; diameter of the octagonal base, 2 5/8 inches. Capacity, about 2 ounces. Fort Laramie, 1880–90.

347 Glue (?) bottle. Transparent, colorless glass with a plain neck finish. Height, 3 1/4 inches; base diameter, 2 1/16 inches. Capacity, about 2 ounces. Fort Laramie, 1880–90.

348 Glue (?) bottle. Transparent, colorless glass with a ring-lip neck finish. Molded inscription around the perimeter of the base: "CARTER'S" and in the center the numerals "157". Height, 2 9/16 inches; base diameter, 2 1/16 inches. Capacity, about 2 ounces. Fort Laramie, 1880–90.

349 Mucilage bottle. Transparent, blue glass with a thickened, plain-lip neck finish. Molded with an inscription on a cylindrical body: "VANSTANS/STRATENA." Height, 2 1/8 inches base diameter, 1 1/4 inches. Capacity, about 1 ounce. Fort Union, 1865–90.

350 Shoe-dressing bottle. Square, polish style. Transparent, colorless glass with a thickened, plain-lip neck finish. Molded with "C / 8" in the base within a circular depression. Height, 4 13/16 inches; base, 1 3/4 × 1 3/4 inches. Capacity, about 6 ounces. Fort Union, 1880–90.

351 Shoe-dressing bottle. Transparent, blue glass with a thickened, plain-lip neck finish. Molded with an inscription on a rectangular body: "FRANK / MILLER'S / CROWN / (crown) / DRESSING / NEW YORK / U.S.A." The remnant of the paper label reads: "CROWN / DRESSING / FOR / LADIES AND / CHILDRENS / ...LT... SHOES" with five additional, illegible lines. The number "5" is inscribed in the center of the square base. Height, 5 1/16 inches; base, 1 3/4 × 1 3/4 inches. Capacity, about 5 ounces. Fort Laramie, 1880–90.

352 Shoe-dressing bottle. Transparent, colorless glass. Molded with an inscription on the rectangular body: "FRANK / MILLER'S / (crown) / DRESSING / NEW YORK / U.S.A." The number "2" is inscribed in the center of the square base. Height, unknown; base, 1 3/4 × 1 3/4 inches. Capacity, about 5 ounces. Fort Laramie, 1880–90.

351

352

353 Shoe-blacking bottle. Transparent, green glass with a broad, sloping-collar neck finish. Molded. A small raised dot appears in the center of the base. Height, 7 7/8 inches; base diameter, 2 5/8 inches. Capacity, about 15 ounces. Fort Laramie, 1880–90.

354 Shoe-blacking (?) bottle. Transparent, amber glass with a broad, sloping-collar neck finish. Molded. Height, 7 7/16 inches; base diameter, 2 5/8 inches. Capacity, about 13 ounces. Fort Laramie, 1880–1900.

353

354

355 Household-oil bottle. Transparent, blue glass with a thickened, plain-lip neck finish. A molded inscription on the body reads: "THREE IN ONE / 3•IN•ONE OIL CO." Centered in the base, parallel with the short axis is "P / 9". Height, 4 1/16 inches; base, 3/4 × 1 9/16 inches. Capacity, about 2 ounces. Fort Laramie, 1885–90.

355

The consumption of ink at a nineteenth-century army post was enormous. The army then, as now, rode on its records. Post, Company, Regimental Returns, General and Special Orders—all combined to produce a virtual blizzard of paper at even the most remote installation. The nineteenth-century army need not take a back seat to any in its production of paperwork. All such work was hand written during the periods of occupancy at Fort Laramie and Fort Union. Ink was supplied in bulk quantities and poured for use into stands and dipping bottles. Examples of both types of containers were found at the two posts.

The absence of decorative glass ink stands is worth noting. While one might expect the quartermaster to have supplied only highly durable and utilitarian containers for ink, it is surprising to find no examples of containers which can be certainly identified as having been owned by individuals. Isolated and ordinarily far from home and family, army people were prodigious letter writers and journal keepers. Personal use of ink must have approached the quantity of that used during duty hours. It would seem, under the circumstances, that ink bottles found at the two posts would not have been so uniform and utilitarian in design. The fact that they are appears to indicate either that a typical cross-section of this type of bottle was not recovered, or that commercial containers possessed such advantage of durability or availability that they were used for private as well as business purposes.

The bottle depicted in Figure 422 is worth special mention. It is made of hard rubber with a finely threaded neck for extra secure closure, and was intended to be portable. Such containers were called "pocket inkstands" in the nineteenth century. At this place where travel and rough conditions were the order of the day, it is strange that more bottles of this type were not found.

The most common bulk ink container at both forts was that made by the Joseph Bourne Pottery for the P. & J. Arnold Ink Company, a London firm. These bottles originally had paper labels, and might have contained black, green, blue or carmine ink. P. & J. Arnold went out of business around 1950, but the Bourne Company continues to produce fine pottery products.

356 Ink bottle. Transparent, colorless glass with a wide, flaring neck finish. A molded, cylindrical body has an inscription near the base: "CARTER'S INK". Height, 2 1/2 inches; base diameter, 2 5/8 inches. Capacity, about 4 ounces. Fort Union, 1865–90.

357 Ink bottle. Transparent, colorless glass with a wide, flaring neck finish. Molded with an inscription on a cylindrical body: "CARTER'S INK". The remnant of the paper label reads: "...(R?)TE...S / ARABIN / COPYRIGHT...3 BY CARTER, ...insm...re & _____." Height, 2 inches; base diameter, 2 3/8 inches. Capacity, about 4 ounces. Fort Union, 1865–90.

356

357

358 Ink bottle. Transparent, blue glass with a flaring-lip neck finish. Molded, conical body. An inscription on the body reads: "JAQUES / CHEMICAL WORKS / CHICAGO." Height, 2 5/8 inches; base diameter, 2 1/2 inches. Capacity, about 3 ounces. Fort Union, 1865–90.

359 Ink bottle. Transparent, colorless glass with a flaring-lip neck finish. Molded with an inscription on a rectangular body: "SANFORD / MFG. Co. / SMCo (monogram)." Height, 3 inches; base, 1 5/8 × 1 5/8 inches. Capacity, about 6 ounces. Fort Union, 1865–90.

358

359

360

361

362

363

364

365

360 Ink bottle. Transparent, blue glass with a bead neck finish. Molded, conical body. The concave base is marked with the inscribed letters "I G Co." Height, 2 7/8 inches; base diameter, 2 1/8 inches. Capacity, about 3 ounces. Fort Union, 1865–90.

361 Ink bottle. Transparent, blue glass with a thickened, plain-lip neck finish. Molded, conical body. A concave base is marked with the inscribed number "4". Height, 2 1/2 inches; base diameter, 2 1/2 inches. Capacity, about 3 ounces. Fort Union, 1865–90.

362 Ink bottle. Transparent, blue glass with an unknown neck finish. Height, unknown; diameter of the 12-sided base, 2 3/8 inches. Capacity, about 3 ounces. Fort Union, 1865–90.

363 Ink bottle. Transparent, blue glass with a thickened, plain-lip neck finish. Height, 2 1/8 inches; diameter of the 12-sided base, 2 1/8 inches. Capacity, about 2 ounces. Fort Union, 1865–90.

364 Ink bottle. Transparent, blue glass with a flaring-lip neck finish. Height, 2 3/8 inches; diameter of the octagonal base, 2 inches. Capacity, about 3 ounces. Fort Union, 1865–90.

365 Ink bottle. Wheel-thrown, cream-colored, salt-glazed stoneware. Height, 4 3/8 inches; base diameter, 1 3/4 inches. Capacity, about 4 ounces. Fort Union, 1863–90.

366 Ink bottle. Cone stand style. Wheel-thrown, brown, salt-glazed stoneware with a double-ring neck finish. Height, 2 1/2 inches; base diameter, 2 7/8 inches. Capacity, about 3 ounces. Fort Union, 1863–90.

367 Ink bottle. Cone stand style. Wheel-thrown, brown, salt-glazed stoneware with a thin-ring neck finish. Height, 2 1/4 inches; base diameter, 1 7/8 inches. Capacity, about 2 ounces. Fort Union, 1863–90.

366

367

368 Ink bottle. Cone stand style. Wheel-thrown, brown, salt-glazed stoneware with a ring neck finish above a narrow ring. Height, 2 5/8 inches; base diameter, 2 3/8 inches. Capacity, about 3 ounces. Fort Union, 1863–90.

369 Ink bottle. Round stand style. Wheel-thrown, brown, salt-glazed stoneware with a ring neck finish above a narrow ring. Height, 1 7/8 inches; base diameter, 2 1/2 inches. Capacity, about 3 ounces. Fort Union, 1863–90.

368

369

370 Ink bottle. Transparent, green glass. Broad, sloping-shoulder neck finish above a narrow ring with a pouring lip. Molded, with an inscription on the shoulder: "CARTER'S". Height, 8 inches; base diameter, 2 1/2 inches. Capacity, about 7 1/2 ounces. Fort Union, 1865–90.

371 Ink bottle. Transparent, pale blue glass with a thickened, plain-lip neck finish. Height, 2 5/8 inches; base diameter, 2 1/2 inches. Capacity, about 3 ounces. Fort Union, 1865–90.

370

371

372

373

372 Ink bottle. Transparent, colorless glass with a flaring-lip neck finish. Height, 4 1/4 inches; base, 1 7/8 × 1 7/8 inches. Capacity, about 7 ounces. Fort Union, 1880–90.

373 Ink bottle. Transparent, colorless glass with a plain neck finish. Height, 2 1/2 inches; base diameter, 2 inches. Capacity, about 4 ounces. Fort Union, 1870–90.

374

375

374 Ink bottle. Salt-glazed, wheel-thrown stoneware. Cylindrical with a thickened, plain-lip neck finish. Height, 4 1/2 inches; base diameter, 1 3/4 inches. Capacity, about 4 ounces. Fort Union, 1865–90.

375 Ink bottle. Transparent, blue glass with a thickened, plain-lip neck finish. Height, 2 3/8 inches; base diameter, 2 1/2 inches. Capacity, about 3 ounces. Fort Union, 1865–90.

376

377

376 Ink bottle. Transparent, blue glass with a thickened, plain-lip neck finish. Height, 2 1/4 inches; base diameter, 2 inches. Capacity, about 1 ounce. Fort Union, 1870–90.

377 Ink bottle. Salt-glazed, wheel-thrown stoneware with a ring-lip neck finish. Height, 2 inches; base diameter, 1 7/8 inches. Capacity, about 1 ounce. Fort Union, 1865–90.

378 Ink bottle. Salt-glazed, wheel-thrown stoneware with a ring-lip neck finish. Height, 2 3/4 inches; base diameter, 2 1/4 inches. Capacity, about 1 ounce. Fort Union, 1880–85.

379 Ink bottle. Transparent, pale green glass with a plain-lip neck finish. Molded with "S S S" on base. Height, 2 1/2 inches; diameter of the octagonal base, 2 1/4 inches. Capacity, about 2 ounces. Fort Union, 1870–90.

378   379

380 Ink bottle. Transparent, blue glass with a poorly executed ring-lip neck finish. Molded with an inscription around the shoulder: "J. J. BUTLER CIN O". Height, 2 1/4 inches; base diameter, 1 5/8 inches. Capacity, about 1 ounce. Fort Laramie, 1860–75.

381 Ink bottle. Transparent, blue glass with a thickened, plain-lip neck finish. Molded with an inscription on a cylindrical body: "J J BUT-LER / CINCINNATI". Height, 2 inches; base diameter, 2 1/8 inches. Capacity, about 1 ounce. Fort Laramie, 1867–75.

380   381

382 Ink bottle. Transparent, colorless glass with a plain, rounded neck finish. Molded, conical body with an inscription around the shoulder: "CARTER'S". Height, 2 7/8 inches; base diameter, 2 9/16 inches. Capacity, about 2 ounces. Fort Laramie, 1870–90.

383 Ink bottle. Transparent, green glass with a plain, rounded-lip neck finish. Molded, conical body. An inscription around the perimeter of the round base reads: "CARTER'S / MAY." Height, 2 1/2 inches; base diameter, 2 1/2 inches. Capacity, about 1 ounce. Fort Laramie, 1875–90.

382   383

384

385

386

387

388

389

384 Ink bottle. Transparent, colorless glass with a plain, rounded-lip neck finish. Molded, conical body. An inscription around the perimeter of the round base reads: "CARTER'S". Centered in the concave base is the number "3". Height, 2 1/2 inches; base diameter, 2 1/2 inches. Capacity, about 1 ounce. Fort Laramie, 1875–90.

385 Ink bottle. Transparent, colorless glass with a plain, rounded-lip neck finish. Molded, conical body. An inscription around the perimeter of the round base reads: "CARTER'S." Centered in the concave base is the number "12". Height, 2 1/2 inches; base diameter, 2 3/8 inches. Capacity, about 3 ounces. Fort Laramie, 1875–90.

386 Ink bottle. Transparent, light-blue glass with a plain-lip neck finish. Molded with an inscription near the base of a cylindrical body: "DESSAUER'S JET BLACK INK." Height, 1 7/8 inches; base diameter, 2 1/8 inches. Capacity, about 1 ounce. Fort Laramie, 1875–90.

387 Ink bottle. Transparent, blue glass with a plain-lip neck finish. Molded, conical body. An inscription around the perimeter of the round base reads: "SANFORD'S." Inscribed in the center of the base is the number "8". Height, 2 3/4 inches; base diameter, 2 1/2 inches. Capacity, about 2 ounces. Fort Laramie, 1875–90.

388 Ink bottle. Transparent, light-blue glass with a thickened, plain-lip neck finish. Molded, conical body. An inscription on the body reads: L. H. THOMAS' / INK". The remaining fragment of the paper label reads: "_____ / B...IN _____ / ...MAS, / ADIN...". Height, 2 5/8 inches; base diameter, 2 7/16 inches. Capacity, about 1 ounce. Fort Laramie, 1870–90.

389 Ink bottle. Transparent, blue glass with a thickened, plain-lip neck finish. Molded with an inscription on a cylindrical body: "VIOLA INK A & F PATD 1872." Height ranges from 1 3/4 inches to 1 7/8 inches; base diameter, 2 1/8 inches. Capacity, about 1 ounce. Fort Laramie, 1872–90.

390 Ink bottle. Cone stand style. Brown, salt-glazed, wheel-thrown stoneware. The neck finish has a thin, ringed lip. Height, 2 7/16 inches; base diameter, 1 13/16 inches. Capacity, about 1 ounce. Fort Laramie, 1865–90.

391 Ink bottle. Brown, salt-glazed, wheel-thrown stoneware with a thin-ring lip. Cylindrical body, round base. Height ranges from 1 7/8 inches to 2 1/16 inches; base diameter, 1 15/16 inches. Capacity, about 1 ounce. Fort Laramie, 1865–90.

390   391

392 Ink bottle. Transparent, colorless glass with a plain-lip finish. Molded, square body with an inscription on the base: "W. T. & CO / 8." Height, 3 inches; base, 1 11/16 × 1 11/16 inches. Capacity, about 1 ounce. Fort Laramie, 1875–90.

393 Ink bottle. Fluted, cone stand style. Transparent, blue glass with a thickened, plain-lip neck finish. Molded, conical, octagonal body. The letters "A & F" are inscribed in the center of the round, concave base. Height, 2 7/16 inches; base diameter, 1 15/16 inches. Capacity, about 1 ounce. Fort Laramie, 1870–90.

392   393

394 Ink bottle. Cream-colored, salt-glazed, wheel-thrown stoneware with a ring-lip neck finish. Conical body, round base. Height, 2 15/16 inches; base diameter, 2 1/16 inches. Capacity, about 1 ounce. Fort Laramie, 1865–90.

395 Ink bottle. Transparent, blue glass with a poorly executed ring-lip neck finish. The base is marked in the center with an irregular circle with irregular lines radiating out to the perimeter of the specimen. Height, 2 11/16 inches; base diameter, 2 1/4 inches. Capacity, about 2 ounces. Fort Laramie, 1870–90.

394   395

396

397

398

399

400

401

396 Ink bottle. Transparent, blue glass with a ring-lip neck finish. Height, 2 3/8 inches; 12-sided base diameter, 2 5/16 inches. Capacity, about 1 ounce. Fort Laramie, 1870–90.

397 Ink bottle. Transparent, blue glass with a ring-lip neck finish. Blown-molded. A rough pontil scar appears in the center of the 12-sided base. Height, 2 1/2 inches; base diameter, 2 3/8 inches. Capacity, about 1 ounce. Fort Laramie, 1855–65.

398 Ink bottle. Transparent, blue glass with a bead-lip neck finish. Height, 2 5/8 inches; diameter of the octagonal base, 2 1/2 inches. Capacity, about 1 ounce. Fort Laramie, 1875–90.

399 Ink bottle. Transparent, blue glass with a thickened, plain-lip neck finish. Height, 2 3/8 inches; diameter of the octagonal base, 1 7/8 inches. Capacity, about 1 ounce. Fort Laramie, 1875–90.

400 Ink bottle. Transparent, colorless glass with a thickened, plain-lip neck finish. Height, 2 7/8 inches; base, 1 11/16 × 1 11/16 inches. Capacity, about 1 ounce. Fort Laramie, 1880–90.

401 Ink bottle. Transparent, blue glass. Height, unknown; base diameter, 2 3/8 inches. Capacity, about 1 ounce. Fort Laramie, 1880–90.

402 Ink bottle. Transparent, colorless glass with a thickened, plain-lip neck finish. The remnant of the paper label reads: "DAVID'S / BRILLIANT / INK / Manufactur(ed) by / _____ / Use a Gold or Quill Pen." Height, 3 inches; base, 1 3/4 × 1 3/4 inches. Capacity, about 1 1/2 ounces. Fort Laramie, 1885–90.

403 Ink (?) bottle. Transparent, colorless glass with a thickened, plain-lip neck finish. Molded with an inscription on a rectangular body: "PERINE / GUYOT / & C'I." Height, 2 13/16 inches; base, 1 3/8 × 1 3/8 inches. Capacity, about 1 ounce. Fort Laramie, 1865–90.

402   403

404 Bulk ink bottle. Brown, salt-glazed, wheel-thrown stoneware. Cylindrical body with a wide, flaring neck finish. An impressed inscription near the base reads: "VITREOUS STONE BOTTLES / J. BOURNE & SON / PATENTEES / Denby & Codnor Park Potters / Near Derby / (incised line) / P. & J. ARNOLD / LONDON". Height, 8 7/8 inches; base diameter, 3 1/2 inches. Capacity, about 27 ounces. Fort Union, 1865–90.

405 Bulk ink bottle. Transparent, blue glass with a wide, flaring neck finish for pouring. Molded with a cylindrical body. An inscription around the shoulder reads: "J. J. BUTLER'S FLUID INKS CINCT. O." Height, 9 7/8 inches; base diameter, 3 1/8 inches. Capacity, about 27 ounces. Fort Union, 1865–90.

404   405

406 Bulk ink bottle. Salt-glazed, wheel-thrown stoneware with a wide, flaring neck finish. An inscription stamped on the body reads: "VITREOUS STONE BOTTLES / WARRENTED [sic] NOT TO / ABSORB. / (incised straight line)". Height, 8 1/8 inches; base diameter, 3 1/2 inches. Capacity, about 22 ounces. Fort Union, 1865–90.

407 Bulk ink bottle. Reddish brown, salt-glazed, wheel-thrown stoneware. Cylindrical with a wide, flaring neck finish for pouring. An impressed inscription on the body reads: "VITREOUS STONE BOTTLE, / J. BOURNE & SON, / PATENTEES, / DENBY POTTERY, / NEAR DERBY, / (long straight line) / P. & J. ARNOLD, / LONDON." Height, 7 1/4 inches; base diameter, 3 inches. Capacity, about 16 ounces. Fort Union, 1863–90.

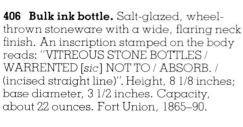

406   407

408

409

408 Bulk ink bottle. Transparent, blue glass with a broad, sloping-collar neck finish. Height, 7 5/8 inches; base diameter, 2 5/8 inches. Capacity, about 13 ounces. Fort Union, 1865–90.

409 Bulk ink bottle. Reddish brown, salt-glazed, wheel-thrown stoneware. Cylindrical with a wide, flaring neck finish. An impressed inscription on the body reads: "VITREOUS STONE BOTTLE, / BOURNE & SON, / PATENTEES, / DENBY POTTERY, / NEAR DERBY, / (long straight line) / P. & J. ARNOLD, / LONDON." Height, 7 inches; base diameter, 3 inches. Capacity, about 15 ounces. Fort Union, 1863–90.

410

411

410 Bulk ink bottle. Salt-glazed, wheel-thrown stoneware. Cylindrical body with a wide, flaring neck finish. Incised horizontal lines occur near the base, about midway on the body, and just above the shoulder. Height, 5 7/8 inches; base diameter, 2 1/2 inches. Capacity, about 7 1/2 ounces. Fort Union, 1863–90.

411 Bulk ink bottle. Brown, unglazed, wheel-thrown stoneware. Wide, flaring neck finish. Height, 9 inches; base diameter, 3 3/8 inches. Capacity, about 24 ounces. Fort Union, 1863–90.

412

413

412 Bulk ink bottle. Brown, salt-glazed, wheel-thrown stoneware. Cylindrical with a wide, flaring neck finish for pouring. An impressed inscription near the base reads: "VITREOUS STONE BOTTLE / J. BOURNE & SON, / PATENTEES / DENBY POTTERY, / NEAR DERBY. / (incised line) / P. & J. ARNOLD / LONDON." Height, 7 inches; base diameter, 3 inches. Capacity, about 16 ounces. Fort Laramie, 1865–90.

413 Bulk ink bottle. Brown, salt-glazed, wheel-thrown stoneware. Cylindrical with wide flaring neck finish for pouring. An impressed inscription near the base reads: "VITREOUS STONE BOTTLE / J. BOURNE & SON, / PATENTEES / DENBY POTTERY, / NEAR DERBY. / (incised line) / P. & J. ARNOLD / LONDON." Height, 8 7/8 inches; base diameter, 3 3/8 inches. Capacity, about 29 ounces. Fort Laramie, 1865–90.

414 Bulk ink bottle. Transparent, blue glass. Molded, cylindrical body. The neck finish has a spouted, broad, sloping collar. Inscribed around the shoulder is "CARTER'S". Height, 9 15/16 inches; base diameter, 3 1/8 inches. Capacity, about 27 ounces. Fort Laramie, 1875–90.

415 Bulk ink bottle. Transparent, green glass. Molded with a spouted neck finish on a cylindrical body. Inscribed around the shoulder is CARTER'S". Height, 8 inches; base diameter, 2 5/8 inches. Capacity, about 16 ounces. Fort Laramie, 1875–90.

414 415

416 Bulk ink bottle. Brown, unglazed, wheel-thrown stoneware with a wide, flaring neck finish. Cylindrical body. Height, 8 1/8 inches; base diameter, 3 inches. Capacity, about 18 ounces. Fort Laramie, 1865–90.

417 Bulk ink bottle. Transparent, green glass with a broad, spouted, sloping-collar neck finish. A raised dot appears in the center of the base. Height, 8 1/8 inches; base diameter, 2 5/8 inches. Capacity, about 16 ounces. Fort Laramie, 1880–90.

416 417

418 Inkwell. Transparent, colorless glass with a plain neck finish. Height, 1 7/16 inches; base, 1 3/8 × 1 3/8 inches. Capacity, about 1 ounce. Fort Union, 1865–90.

419 Inkwell. Transparent, blue glass with a plain neck finish. The base is partly round, partly faceted. A body design, limited to a narrow zone near the base, occurs on each of six facets but does not encircle the specimen. Height, 1 11/16 inches; base diameter, 2 5/16 inches. Capacity, about 1 ounce. Fort Laramie, 1875–90.

418 419

420

421

422

420 Inkwell. Transparent, blue glass with a plain neck finish. Height, 1 5/8 inches; base diameter, 2 3/16 inches. Capacity, about 1 ounce. Fort Laramie, 1880–90.

421 Inkstand. Twelve-sided body. Transparent, blue glass with a thickened, plain-lip neck finish. Height, 2 5/8 inches; base diameter, 2 3/8 inches. Capacity, about 3 ounces. Fort Union, 1865–75.

422 Ink bottle. Pocket inkstand style. Black vulcanite with a continuous-thread neck finish. Height, 1 13/16 inches. Capacity, about 3 ounces. Fort Union, 1880–90. An exact duplicate of this bottle was found at Fort Laramie.

Supplementary
Material

BOTTLE SHAPES AND FINISHES

Not to scale

a.	Beer	
b.	Champagne	
c.	Case	
d.	Jo Jo flask	
e.	Shoofly flask	
f.	Union oval flask	
g.	Picnic flask	
h.	Soda water	
i.	Packing	
j.	Round prescription	
k.	Fluted prescription	
l.	Pomade/morphine	
m.	Panel	
n.	Ball neck panel	
o.	Baltimore oval	
p.	Union oval	
q.	Philadelphia oval	
r.	Blake	
s.	Oblong tooth powder	
t.	French square	
u.	Plain oval	
v.	Vial	
w.	Oval castor oil	
x.	Club sauce	
y.	Olive oil	
z.	Olive bottle	
aa.	Eclipse olive oil	
bb.	American square pickle	
cc.	Octagonal peppersauce/spice	
dd.	Gothic peppersauce	
ee.	Square ring peppersauce	
ff.	French barrel mustard	
gg.	Round horseradish	
hh.	Florida water	
ii.	Oval polish	
jj.	Snuff jar	
kk.	Carmine ink	
ll.	Conical ink	
mm.	Round ink	
nn.	Igloo ink	

a. Prescription
b. Champagne

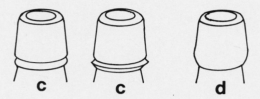

c. Brandy
d. Beer

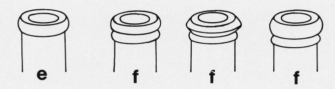

e. Bead
f. Double bead

g. Patent/extract
h. Wide mouth
    patent/extract
i. Oil
j. Packing

k. Crown
l. Club sauce
m. Screw
n. Sheared

Bottle Marks from Fort Union

The line drawings and descriptions on the following pages represent base markings found on beer, bar, and possibly bitters bottles at the last Fort Union (1863–91). The marks are depicted here because the bottles can be dated safely between 1863 and 1891. The dating of Fort Laramie bottles is much more difficult, the result of the long period of occupation by civilians following the army's withdrawal in 1890.

The drawings which follow are approximately half-size. The inscriptions are of corresponding scale. Neck finish descriptions given in the tabulation follow the system of McKearin and McKearin (1948:485–486)* as follows:

Type A—Tooled, plain, broad, sloping collar.
Type B—Tooled, plain, broad, sloping collar with a narrow ring beneath.

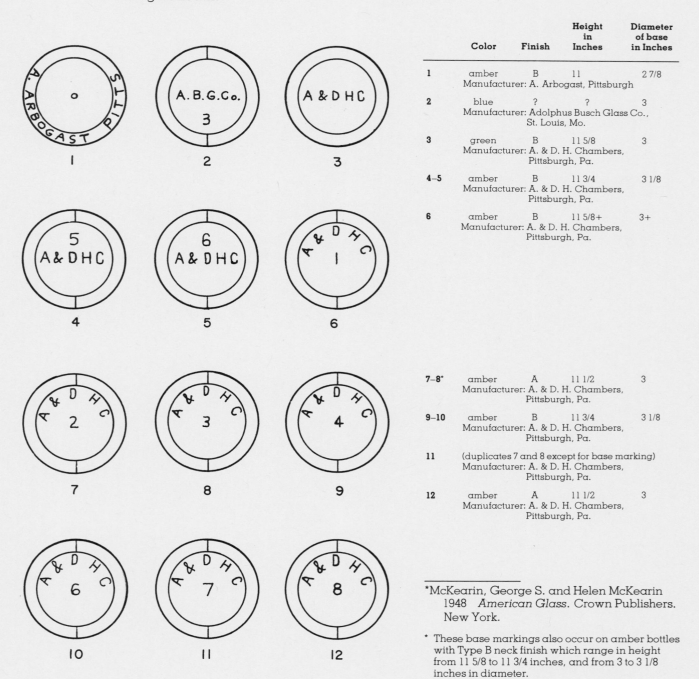

	Color	Finish	Height in Inches	Diameter of base in Inches
1	amber	B	11	2 7/8
	Manufacturer: A. Arbogast, Pittsburgh			
2	blue	?	?	3
	Manufacturer: Adolphus Busch Glass Co., St. Louis, Mo.			
3	green	B	11 5/8	3
	Manufacturer: A. & D. H. Chambers, Pittsburgh, Pa.			
4–5	amber	B	11 3/4	3 1/8
	Manufacturer: A. & D. H. Chambers, Pittsburgh, Pa.			
6	amber	B	11 5/8+	3+
	Manufacturer: A. & D. H. Chambers, Pittsburgh, Pa.			
7–8*	amber	A	11 1/2	3
	Manufacturer: A. & D. H. Chambers, Pittsburgh, Pa.			
9–10	amber	B	11 3/4	3 1/8
	Manufacturer: A. & D. H. Chambers, Pittsburgh, Pa.			
11	(duplicates 7 and 8 except for base marking)			
	Manufacturer: A. & D. H. Chambers, Pittsburgh, Pa.			
12	amber	A	11 1/2	3
	Manufacturer: A. & D. H. Chambers, Pittsburgh, Pa.			

*McKearin, George S. and Helen McKearin
1948 *American Glass*. Crown Publishers. New York.

* These base markings also occur on amber bottles with Type B neck finish which range in height from 11 5/8 to 11 3/4 inches, and from 3 to 3 1/8 inches in diameter.

	Color	Finish	Height in Inches	Diameter of base in Inches
13	amber	B	11 3/4	3 1/8
Manufacturer: A. & D. H. Chambers, Pittsburgh, Pa.				
14	green	B	?	2 3/4
Manufacturer: A. & D. H. Chambers, Pittsburgh, Pa.				
15	amber	?	?	3 1/4
Manufacturer: A. & D. H. Chambers, Pittsburgh, Pa.				
16	amber	?	?	3
Manufacturer: ?				
17–19	amber	B	11 3/4	3
Manufacturer: ?				
20*	amber	B	11 3/4	3
Manufacturer: Cunningham & Co. Pittsburgh, Pa.				
21	amber	B	11 1/4	2 7/8
Manufacturer: ?				
22†	blue	B	11 11/16	3
Manufacturer: ?				
23‡	blue	B	11 7/8	3
Manufacturer: ?				
24	blue	B	11 7/8	3
Manufacturer: ?				
25§	blue	B	11 5/16	2 7/8
Manufacturer: ?				
26	blue	B	11 1/4	3
Manufacturer: ?				
27	amber	B	11 3/8	3
Manufacturer: Cunningham & Ihmsen, Pittsburgh, Pa.				
28	amber	?	?	3
Manufacturer: ?				
29	amber	?	?	3
Manufacturer: ?				
30	amber	?	?	3
Manufacturer: ?				

* This base marking also occurs on amber bottles with Type A neck finish which have a height of 11 3/4 inches and a diameter of 3 inches.

† Molded body inscription: C. Conrad & Co's / Original / BUDWEISER / U.S. Patent No. 6376. C. Conrad's monogram on base.

‡ Molded body inscription: C. CONRAD & COS / ORIGINAL BUDWEISER / U.S. PATENT Nº 6376. C. Conrad's monogram on base.

§ This base marking also occurs on light-blue bottles with Type B neck finish that have a height of 11 1/4 inches and a diameter of 3 inches.

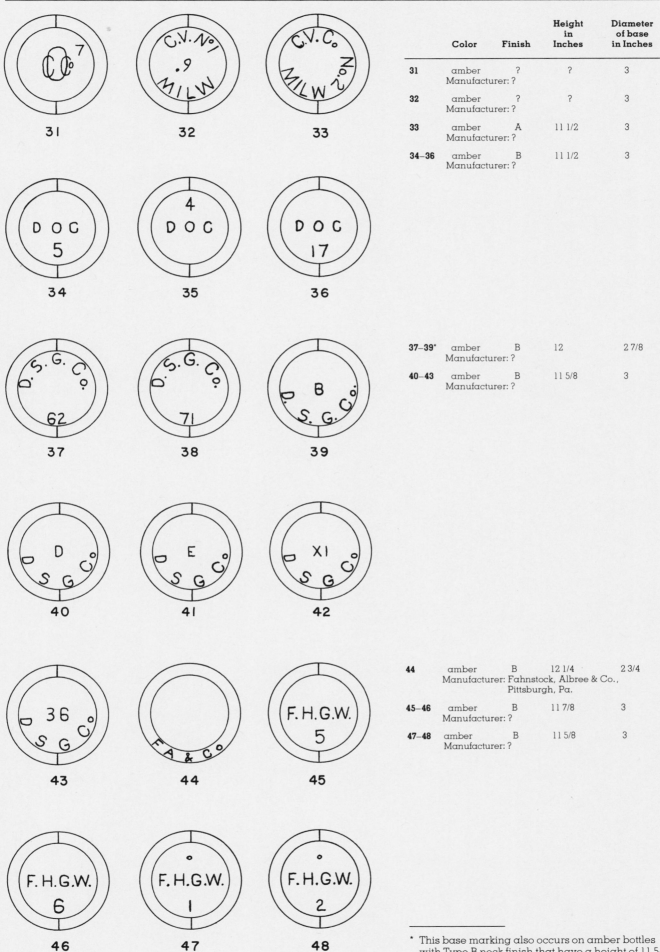

	Color	Finish	Height in Inches	Diameter of base in Inches
31	amber	?	?	3
	Manufacturer: ?			
32	amber	?	?	3
	Manufacturer: ?			
33	amber	A	11 1/2	3
	Manufacturer: ?			
34–36	amber	B	11 1/2	3
	Manufacturer: ?			

	Color	Finish	Height in Inches	Diameter of base in Inches
37–39*	amber	B	12	2 7/8
	Manufacturer: ?			
40–43	amber	B	11 5/8	3
	Manufacturer: ?			

	Color	Finish	Height in Inches	Diameter of base in Inches
44	amber	B	12 1/4	2 3/4
	Manufacturer: Fahnstock, Albree & Co., Pittsburgh, Pa.			
45–46	amber	B	11 7/8	3
	Manufacturer: ?			
47–48	amber	B	11 5/8	3
	Manufacturer: ?			

* This base marking also occurs on amber bottles with Type B neck finish that have a height of 11 5/8 inches and a diameter of 3 inches.

	Color	Finish	Height in Inches	Diameter of Base in Inches
49–65	amber	B	11 5/8	3
	Manufacturer: ?			

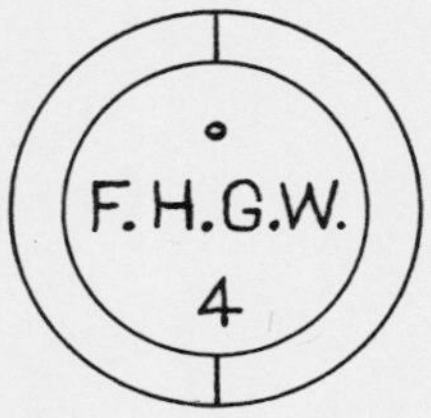

F. H.G.W. 4

49

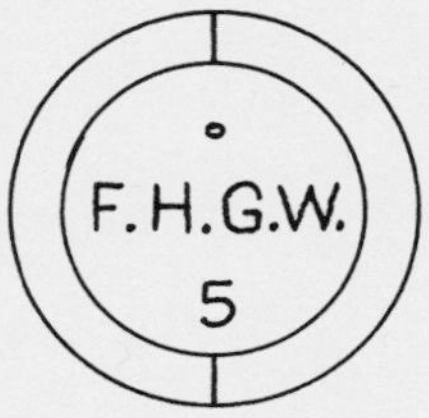

F. H.G.W. 5

50

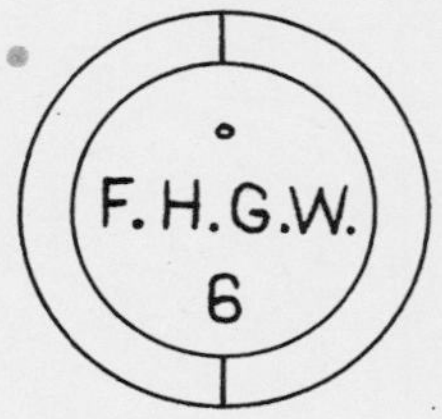

F. H.G.W. 6

51

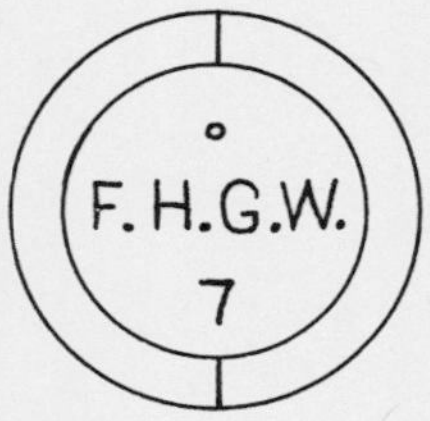

F. H.G.W. 7

52

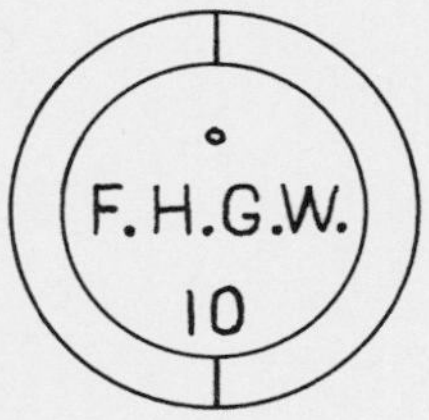

F. H.G.W. 10

53

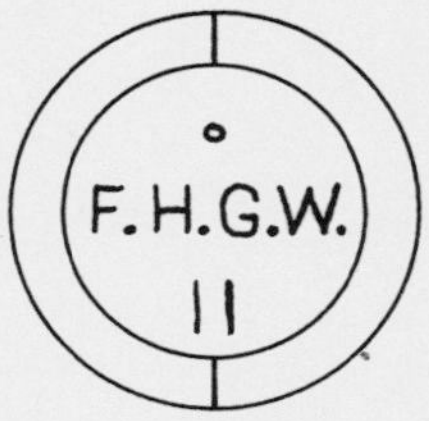

F. H.G.W. 11

54

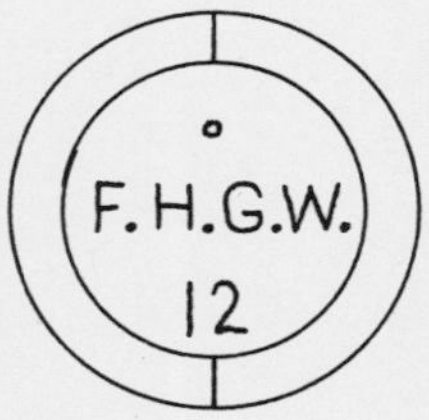

F. H.G.W. 12

55

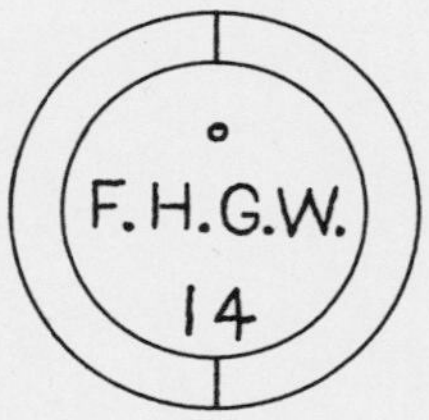

F. H.G.W. 14

56

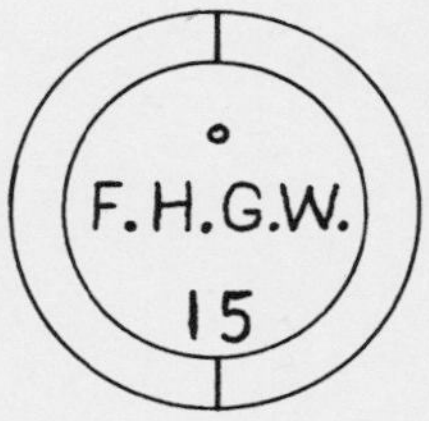

F. H.G.W. 15

57

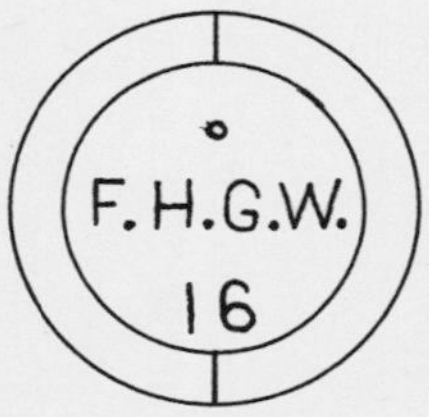

F. H.G.W. 16

58

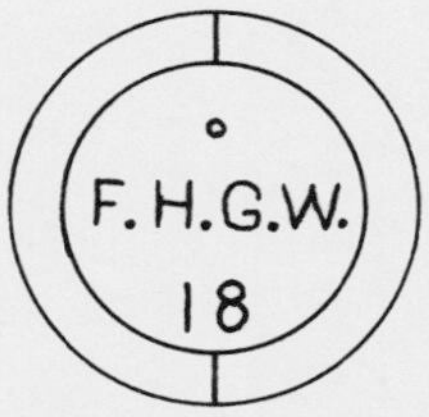

F. H.G.W. 18

59

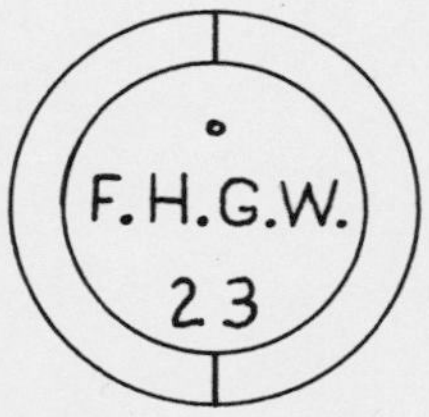

F. H.G.W. 23

60

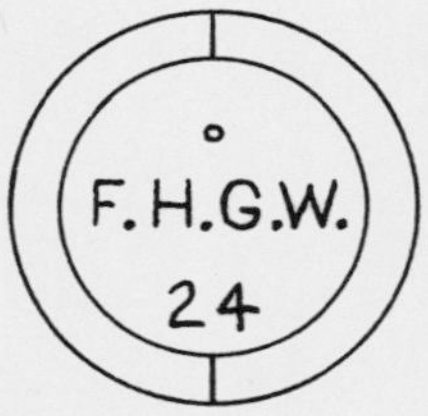

F. H.G.W. 24

61

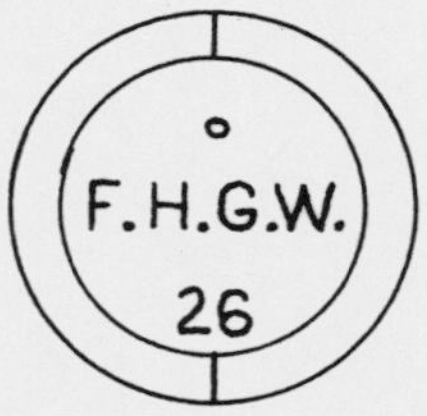

F. H.G.W. 26

62

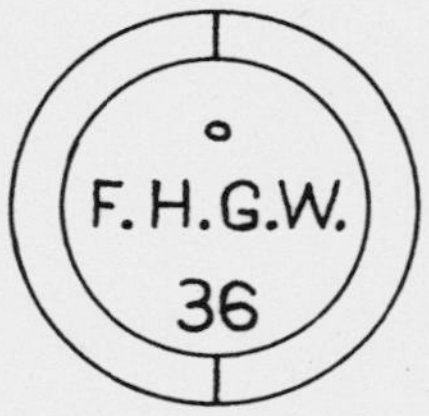

F. H.G.W. 36

63

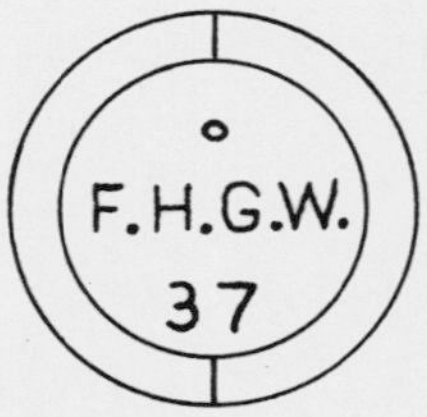

	Color	Finish	Height in Inches	Diameter of Base in Inches
66	amber	?	10 7/8	3
	Manufacturer: ?			

F. H.G.W. 37

64

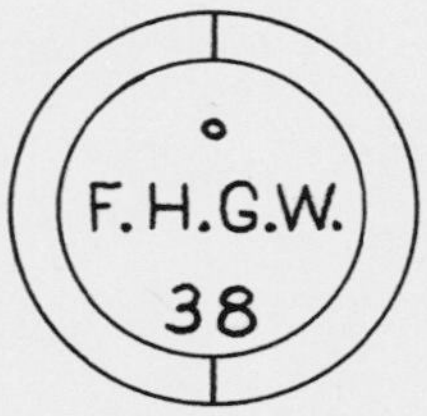

F. H.G.W. 38

65

F H G W 2

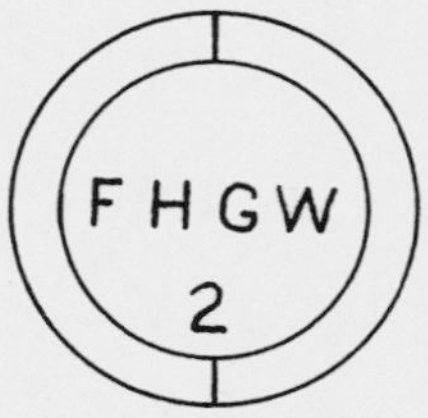

66

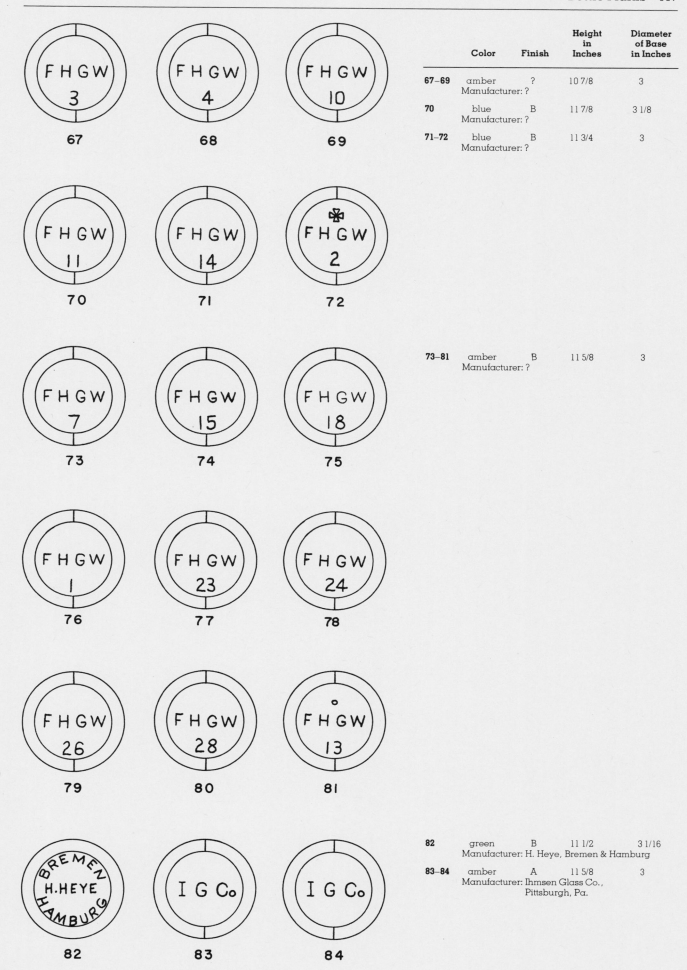

	Color	Finish	Height in Inches	Diameter of Base in Inches
67–69	amber	?	10 7/8	3
	Manufacturer: ?			
70	blue	B	11 7/8	3 1/8
	Manufacturer: ?			
71–72	blue	B	11 3/4	3
	Manufacturer: ?			
73–81	amber	B	11 5/8	3
	Manufacturer: ?			
82	green	B	11 1/2	3 1/16
	Manufacturer: H. Heye, Bremen & Hamburg			
83–84	amber	A	11 5/8	3
	Manufacturer: Ihmsen Glass Co., Pittsburgh, Pa.			

	Color	Finish	Height in Inches	Diameter of Base in Inches
85–86		A	11 5/8	3
Manufacturer: Ihmsen Glass Co., Pittsburgh, Pa.				
87	amber	?	?	?
Manufacturer: H. Heye, Bremen				
88–91	amber	A	11 5/8	3
Manufacturer: Ihmsen Glass Co., Pittsburgh, Pa.				
92–95	amber	B	11 3/4	3
Manufacturer: ?				
96	amber	?	?	3
Manufacturer: ?				
97	green	?	?	2 13/16
Manufacturer: C. Ihmsen Glass Co. Pittsburgh, Pa.				
98–100	amber	B	11 7/8	3
Manufacturer: ?				
101	blue	?	?	3
Manufacturer: ?				
102	blue	?	?	3

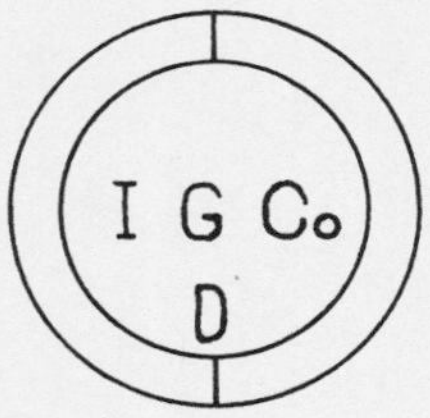

85 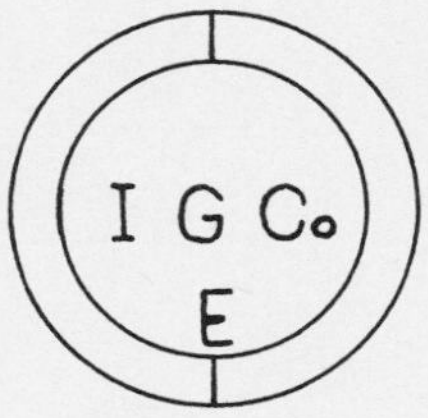   86    87

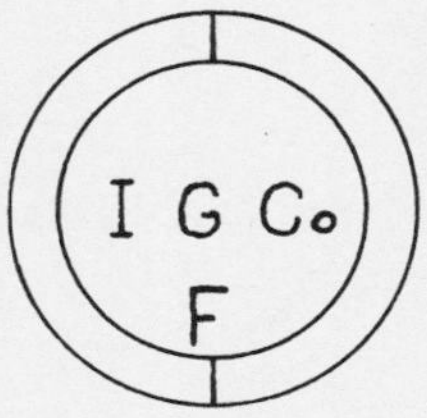

88 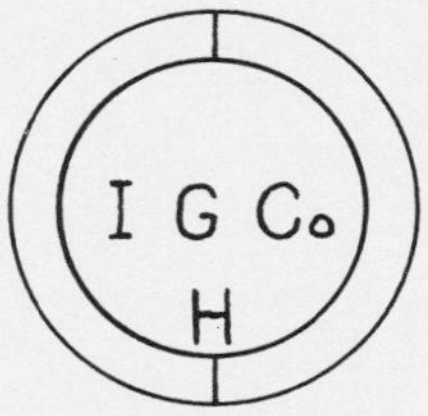   89 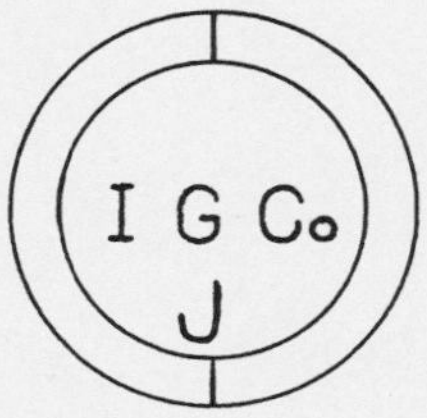   90

91 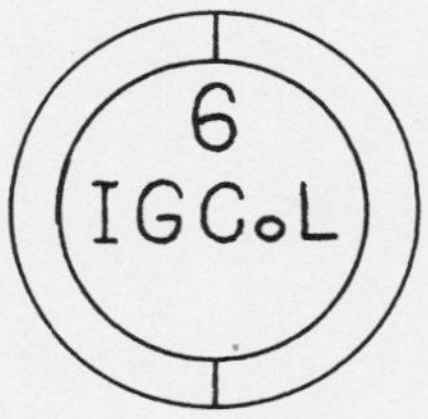   92    93

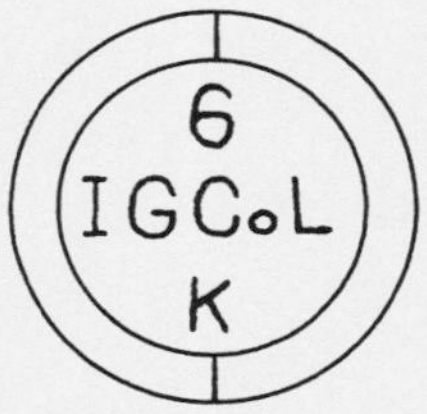

94 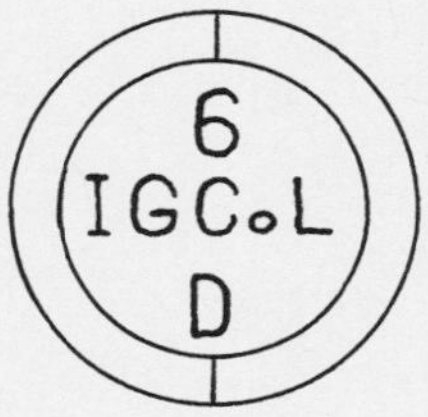   95    96

97    98    99

100    101    102

	Color	Finish	Height in Inches	Diameter of Base in Inches
103–106	amber	A	9 3/4	2 1/2
	Manufacturer: ?			
107–121	amber	B	11 3/4+	3
	Manufacturer: ?			

	Color	Finish	Height in Inches	Diameter of Base in Inches
122–135	amber	B	11 3/4+	3
	Manufacturer: ?			

LGCo 16
121

LGCo 17
122

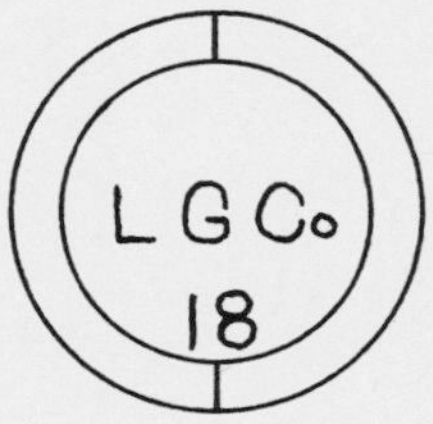

LGCo 18
123

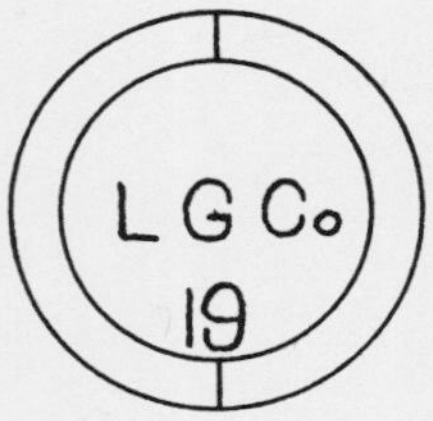

LGCo 19
124

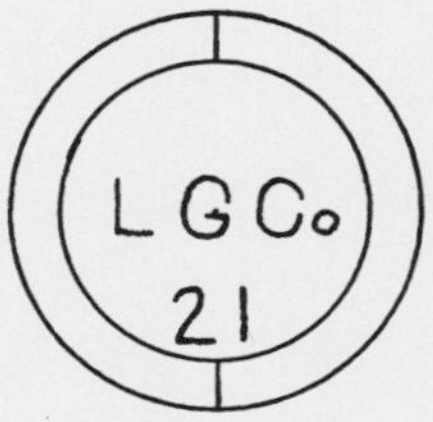

LGCo 21
125

LGCo 23
126

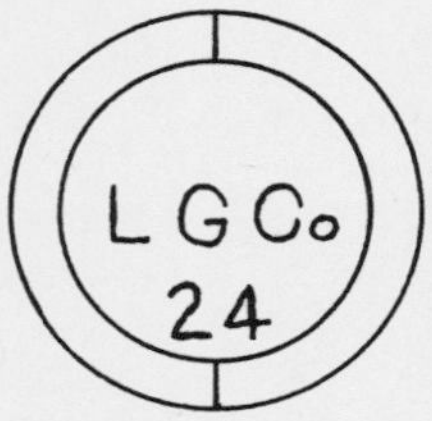

LGCo 24
127

LGCo 25
128

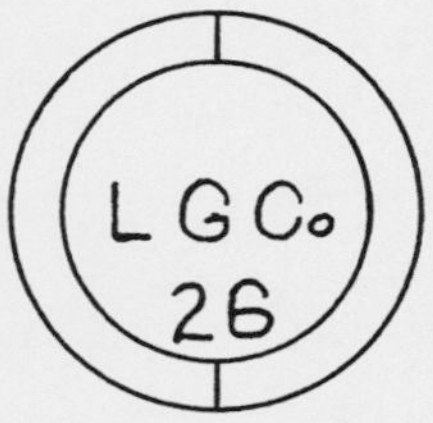

LGCo 26
129

LGCo 27
130

LGCo 36
131

LGCo 38
132

LGCo 15
133

LGCo 19
134

LGCo 20
135

	Color	Finish	Height in Inches	Diameter of Base in Inches
136–138	amber	B	9 1/2	2 1/2
	Manufacturer: ?			

LGCº 1
136

LGCº 15
137

LGCº 17
138

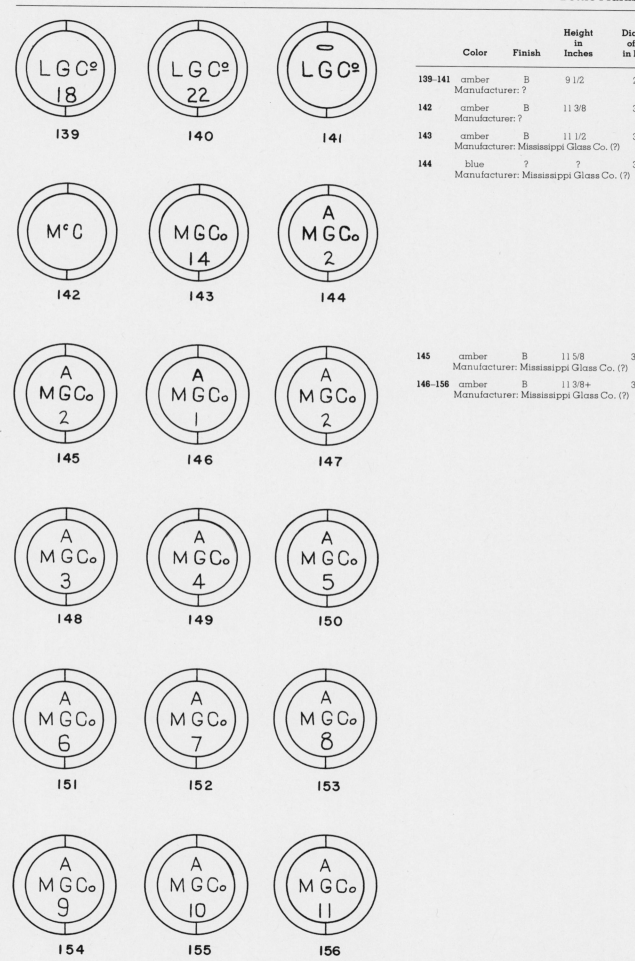

	Color	Finish	Height in Inches	Diameter of Base in Inches
139–141	amber	B	9 1/2	2 1/2
Manufacturer: ?				
142	amber	B	11 3/8	3
Manufacturer: ?				
143	amber	B	11 1/2	3
Manufacturer: Mississippi Glass Co. (?)				
144	blue	?	?	3
Manufacturer: Mississippi Glass Co. (?)				

	Color	Finish	Height in Inches	Diameter of Base in Inches
145	amber	B	11 5/8	3
Manufacturer: Mississippi Glass Co. (?)				
146–156	amber	B	11 3/8+	3
Manufacturer: Mississippi Glass Co. (?)				

	Color	Finish	Height in Inches	Diameter of Base in Inches
157–163	amber	B	11 3/8+	3

Manufacturer: Mississippi Glass Co. (?)

	Color	Finish	Height in Inches	Diameter of Base in Inches
164–167	amber	B	9 1/2	2 1/2

Manufacturer: Mississippi Glass Co. (?)

	Color	Finish	Height in Inches	Diameter of Base in Inches
168–174	blue	B	11 1/4+	3

Manufacturer: Mississippi Glass Co. (?)

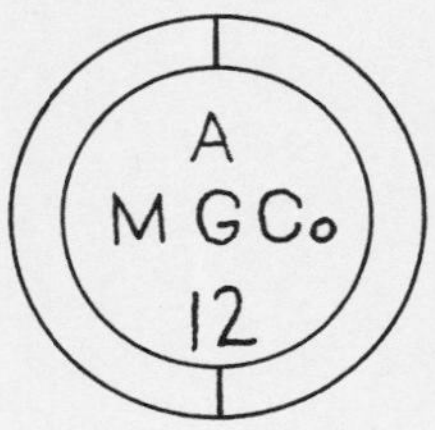

157 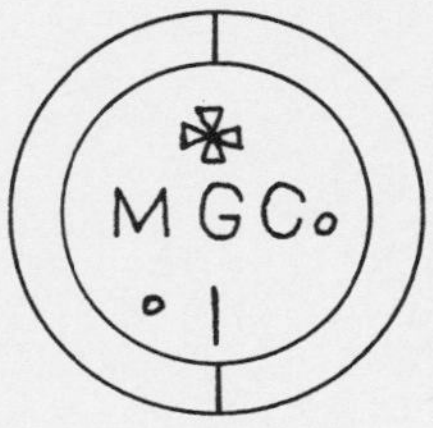   158 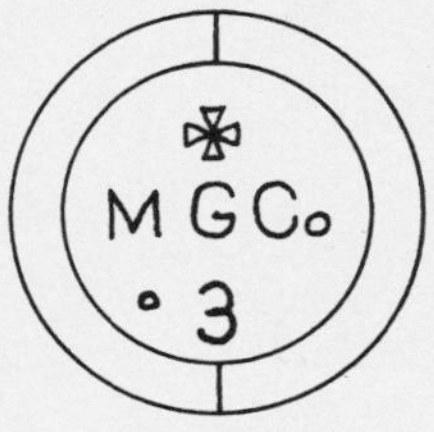   159

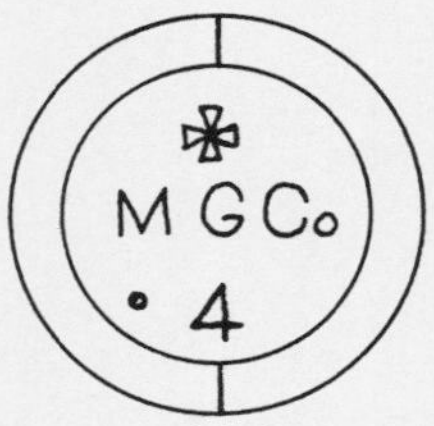

160 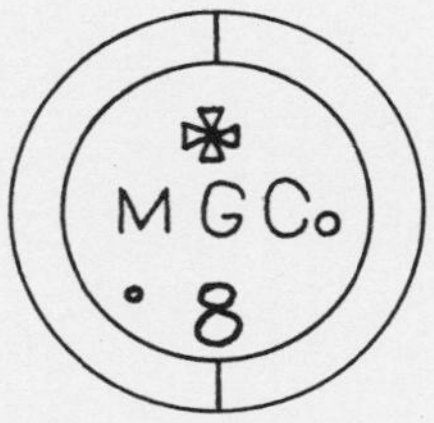   161 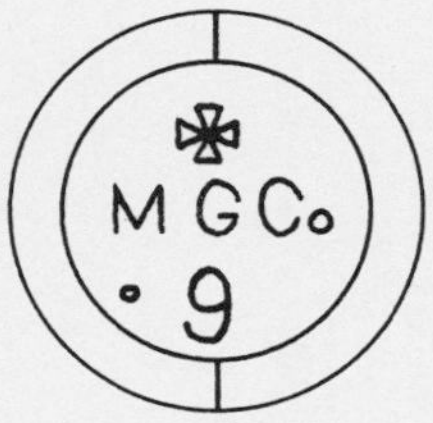   162

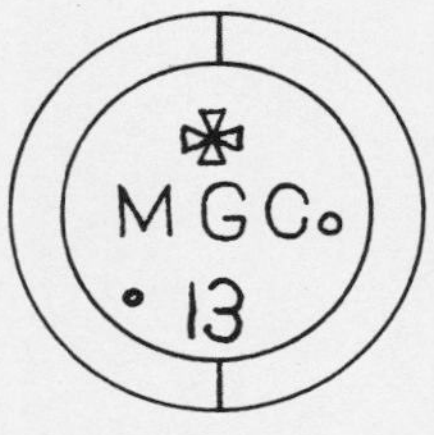

163 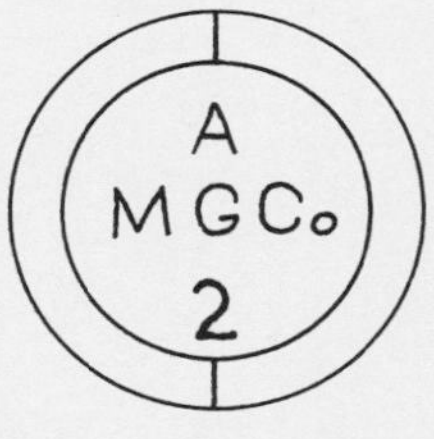   164    165

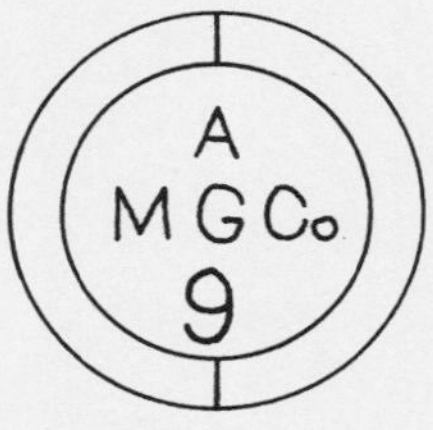

166 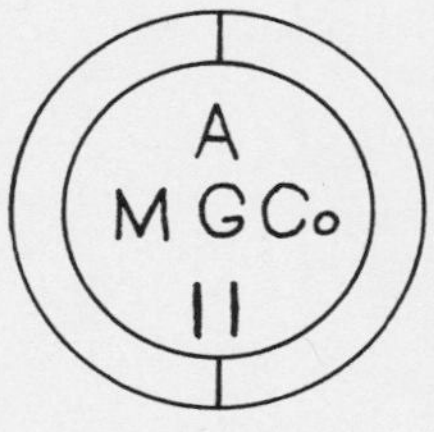   167 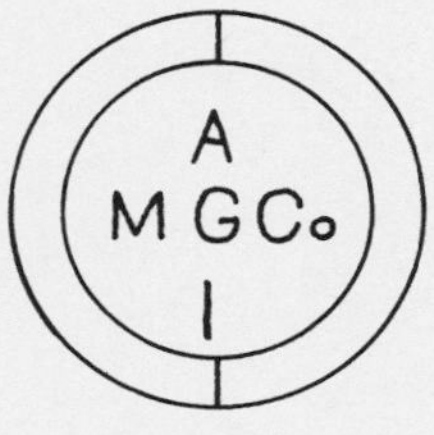   168

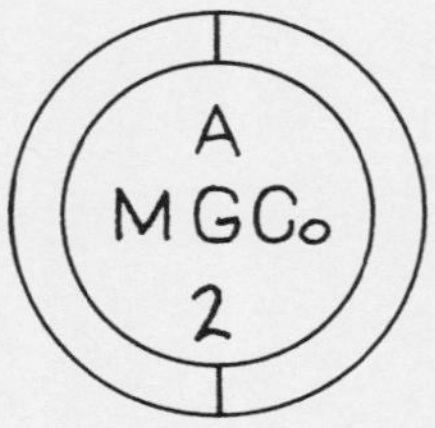

169 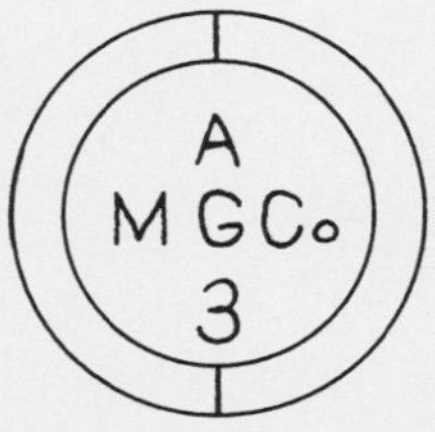   170 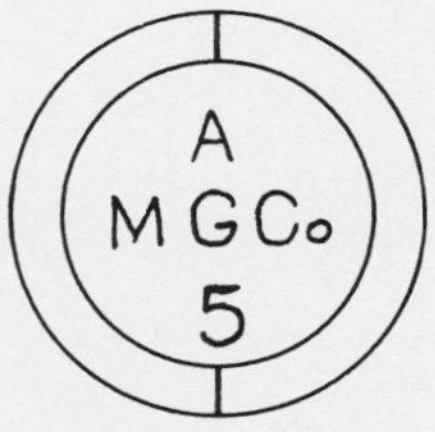   171

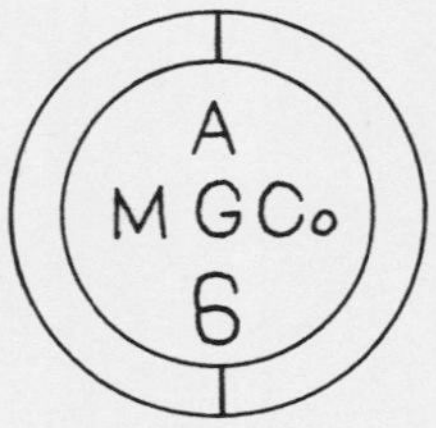

172 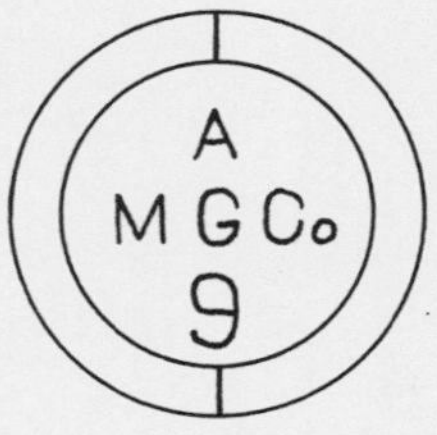   173 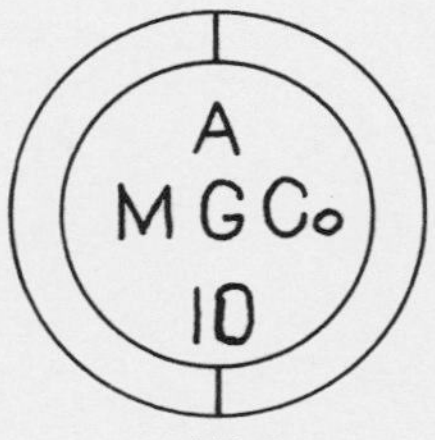   174

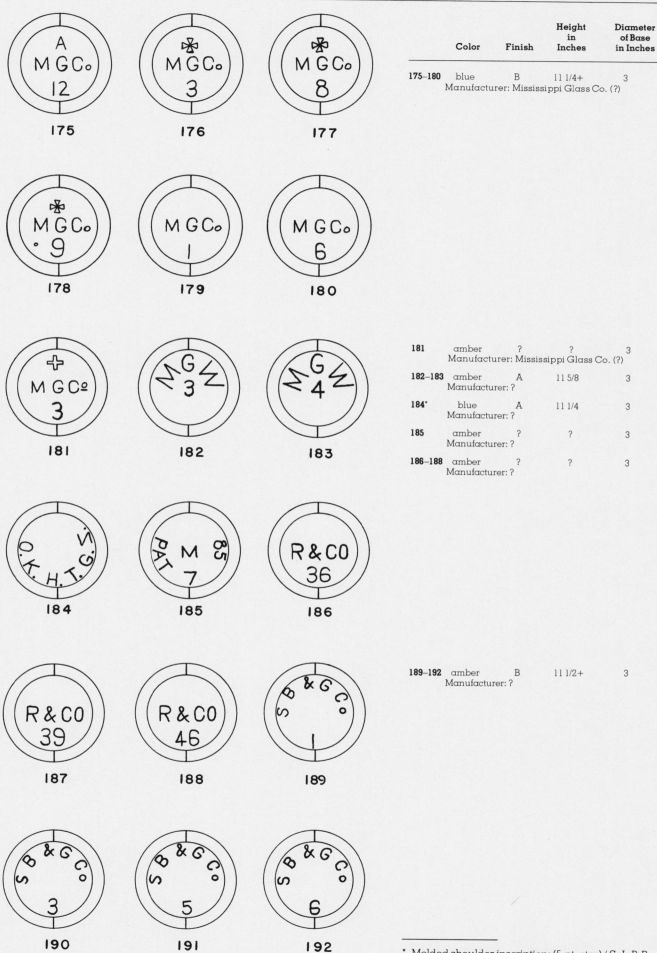

	Color	Finish	Height in Inches	Diameter of Base in Inches
175–180	blue	B	11 1/4+	3
	Manufacturer: Mississippi Glass Co. (?)			

	Color	Finish	Height in Inches	Diameter of Base in Inches
181	amber	?	?	3
	Manufacturer: Mississippi Glass Co. (?)			
182–183	amber	A	11 5/8	3
	Manufacturer: ?			
184*	blue	A	11 1/4	3
	Manufacturer: ?			
185	amber	?	?	3
	Manufacturer: ?			
186–188	amber	?	?	3
	Manufacturer: ?			

	Color	Finish	Height in Inches	Diameter of Base in Inches
189–192	amber	B	11 1/2+	3
	Manufacturer: ?			

* Molded shoulder inscription: (5-pt. star) / S. L.B.B. Co.

	Color	Finish	Height in Inches	Diameter of Base in Inches
193–194	amber	A	11 1/2	3
Manufacturer: ?				
195–202	amber	A	11 5/8	3
Manufacturer: ?				

203–204	amber	?	?	3
Manufacturer: ?				

205–207	amber	A	11 7/8	3
Manufacturer: S. McKee & Co., Pittsburgh, Pa.				
208	blue	?	?	3 1/8
Manufacturer: ?				
209–210	amber	A	11 1/2	3
Manufacturer: Wisconsin Glass Co., Milwaukee				

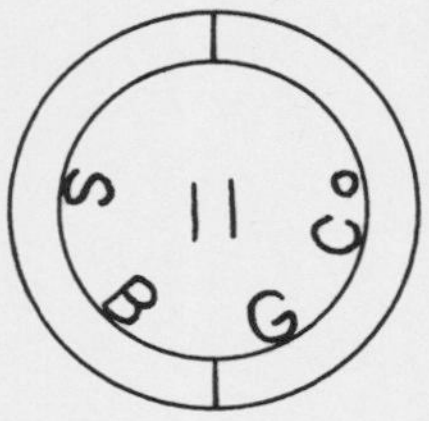

193    194 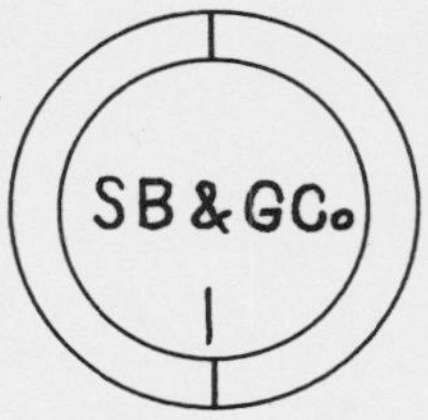   195

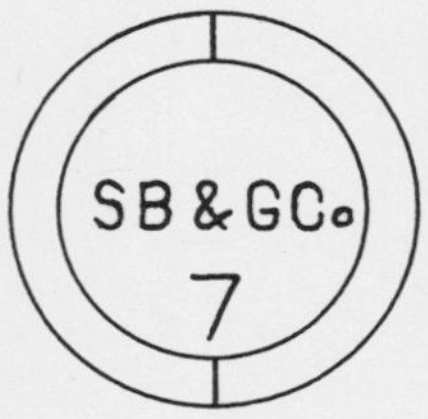

196 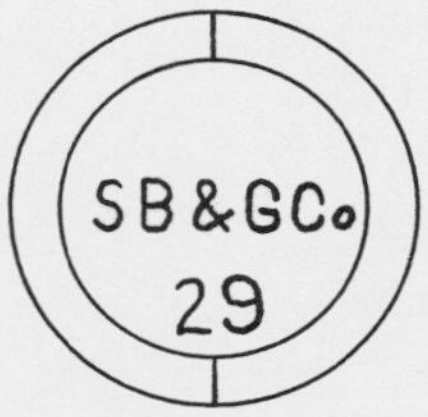   197 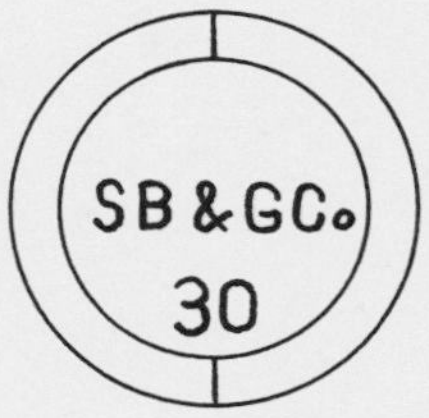   198

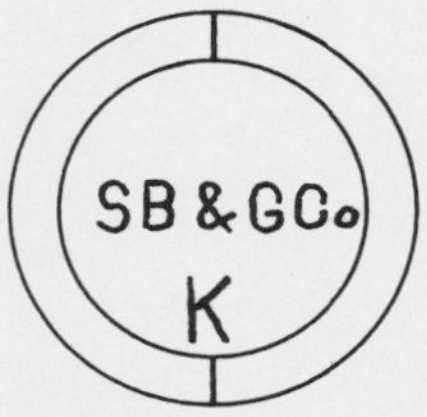

199 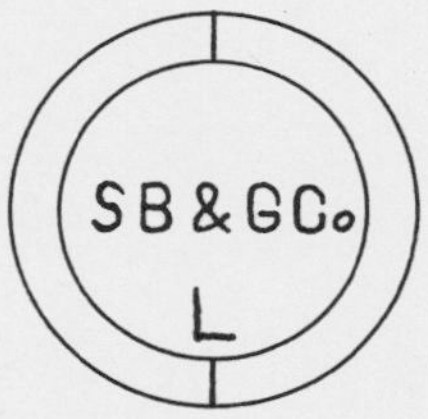   200 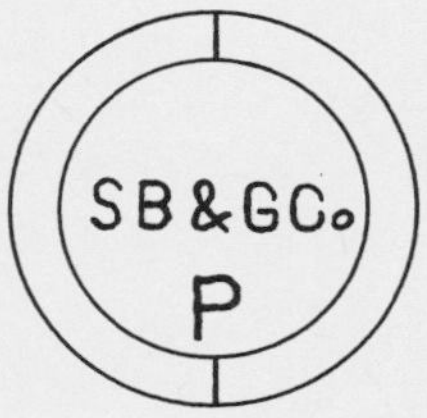   201

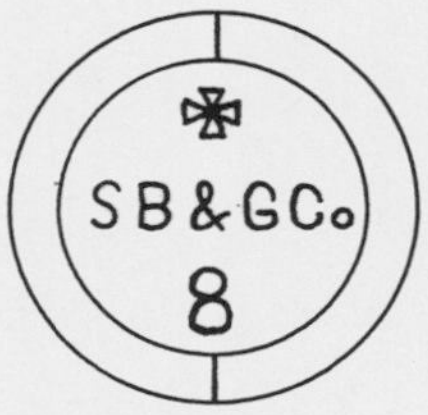

202 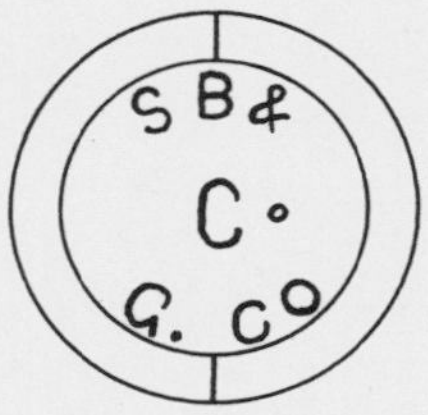   203 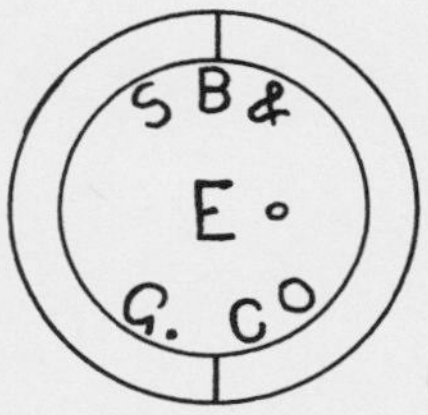   204

205    206    207

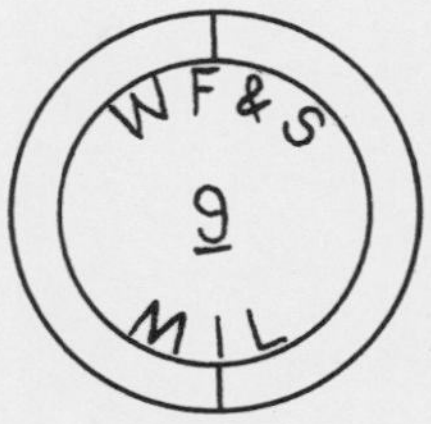

208    209    210

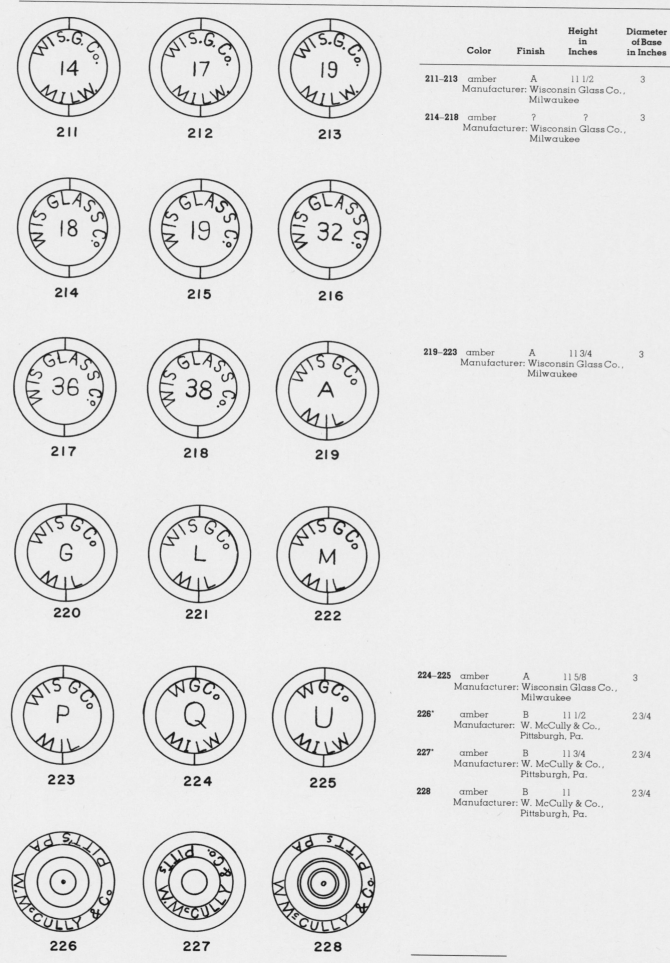

	Color	Finish	Height in Inches	Diameter of Base in Inches
211–213	amber	A	11 1/2	3
Manufacturer: Wisconsin Glass Co., Milwaukee				
214–218	amber	?	?	3
Manufacturer: Wisconsin Glass Co., Milwaukee				
219–223	amber	A	11 3/4	3
Manufacturer: Wisconsin Glass Co., Milwaukee				
224–225	amber	A	11 5/8	3
Manufacturer: Wisconsin Glass Co., Milwaukee				
226*	amber	B	11 1/2	2 3/4
Manufacturer: W. McCully & Co., Pittsburgh, Pa.				
227*	amber	B	11 3/4	2 3/4
Manufacturer: W. McCully & Co., Pittsburgh, Pa.				
228	amber	B	11	2 3/4
Manufacturer: W. McCully & Co., Pittsburgh, Pa.				

* Molded shoulder inscription: PATENT

	Color	Finish	Height in Inches	Diameter of Base in Inches
229*	amber	B	11 7/8	3 1/4
Manufacturer: W. McCully & Co., Pittsburgh, Pa.				
230	amber	B	11 1/2	2 3/4
Manufacturer: W. McCully & Co., Pittsburgh, Pa.				
231–234	amber	B	11 1/2	3
Manufacturer: ?				
235–241	amber	B	11 5/8	2 7/8
Manufacturer: ?				

	Color	Finish	Height in Inches	Diameter of Base in Inches
242	amber	A	11 5/8	2 7/8
Manufacturer: ?				
243	green	B	11 3/8	3
Manufacturer: ?				
244–245	amber	A	11 7/8	2 7/8
Manufacturer: ?				
246	amber	B	?	3
Manufacturer: ?				

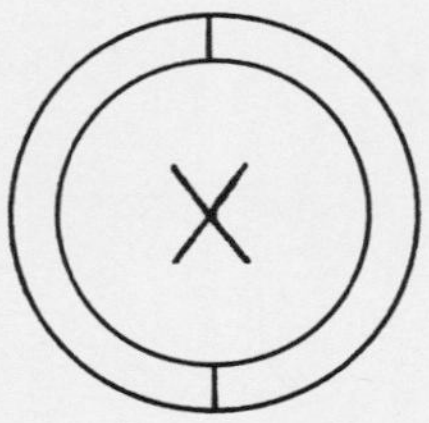

*Molded shoulder inscription: PATENT

229 230 231
232 233 234
235 236 237
238 239 240
241 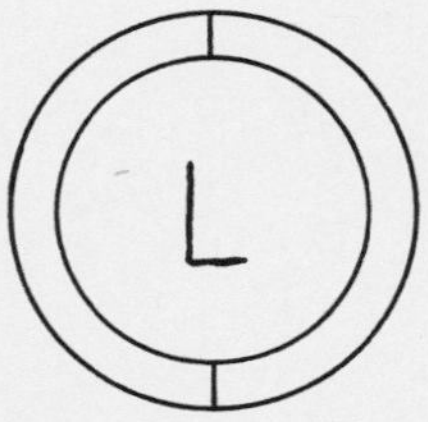 242 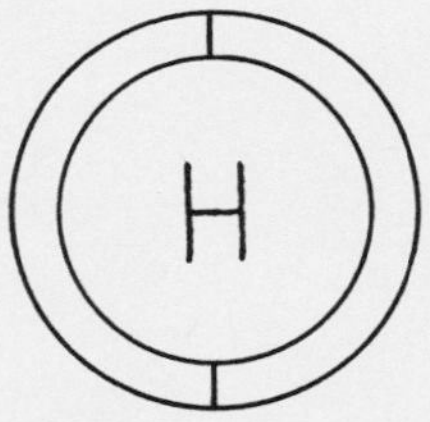 243
244 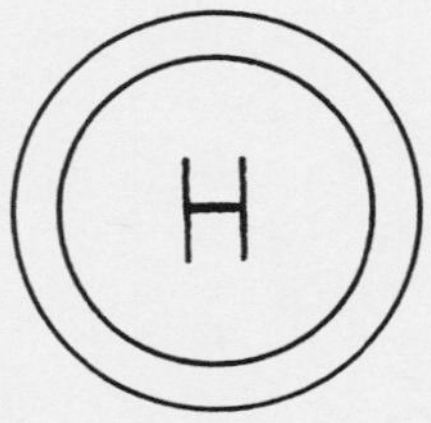 245 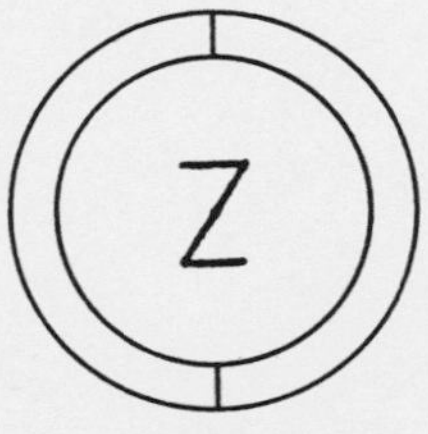 246

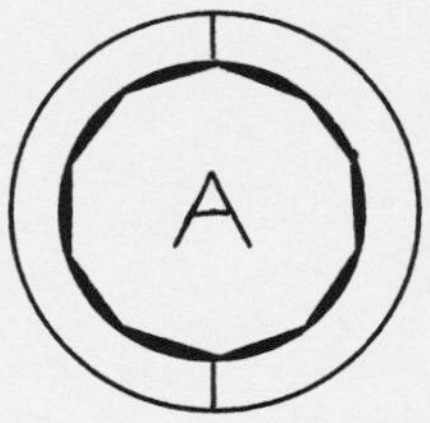

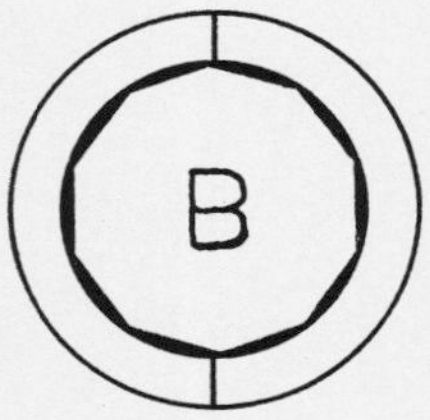

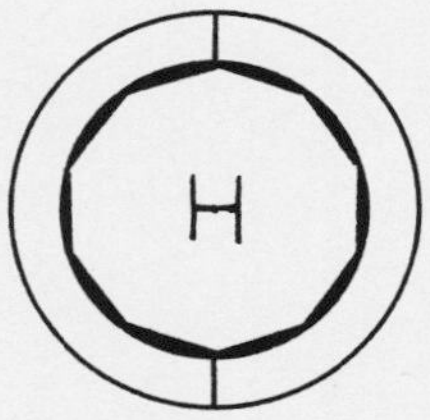

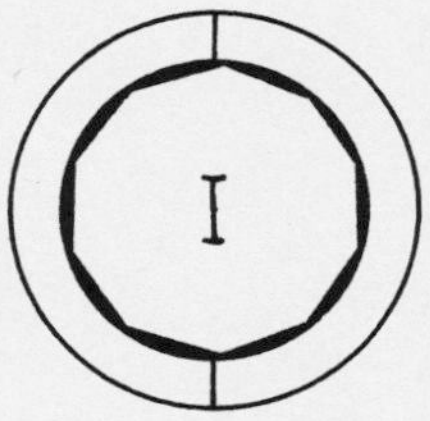

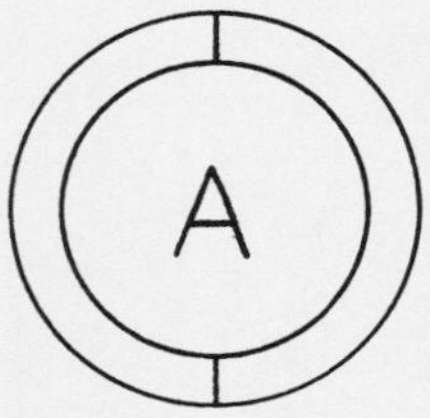

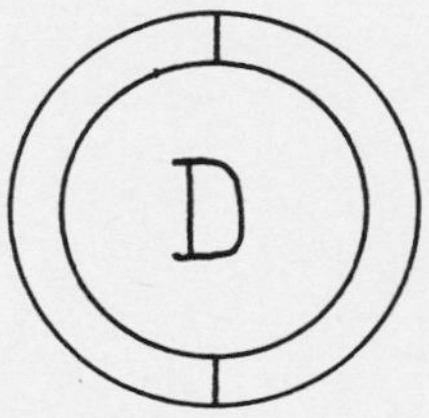

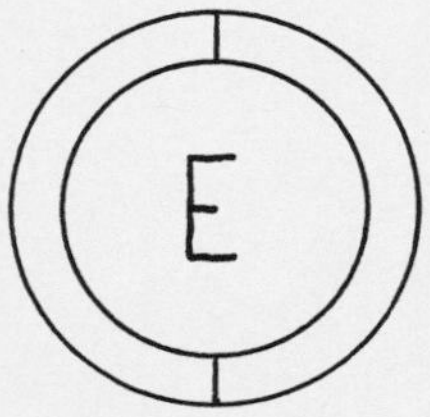

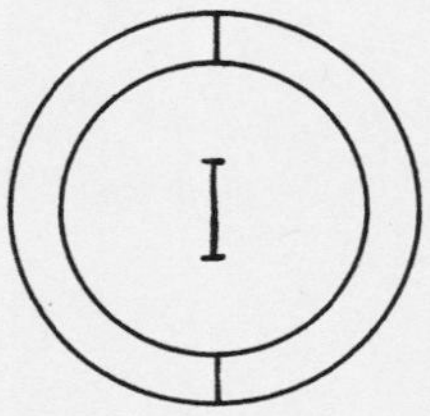

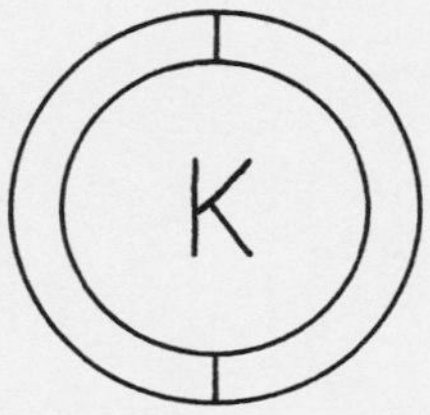

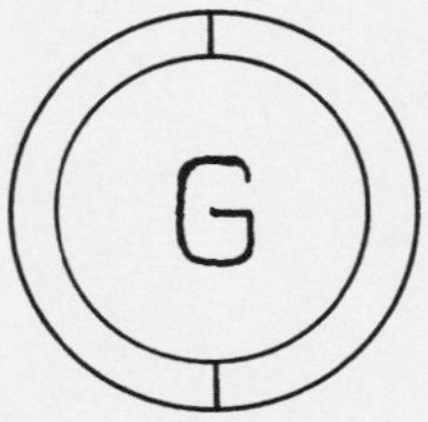

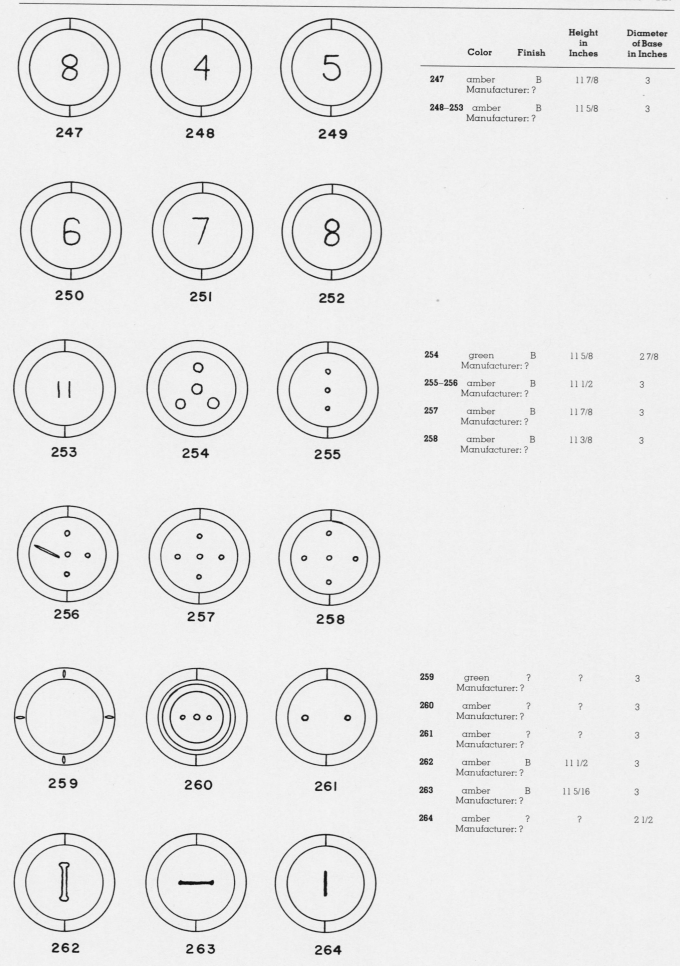

	Color	Finish	Height in Inches	Diameter of Base in Inches
247	amber	B	11 7/8	3
	Manufacturer: ?			
248–253	amber	B	11 5/8	3
	Manufacturer: ?			
254	green	B	11 5/8	2 7/8
	Manufacturer: ?			
255–256	amber	B	11 1/2	3
	Manufacturer: ?			
257	amber	B	11 7/8	3
	Manufacturer: ?			
258	amber	B	11 3/8	3
	Manufacturer: ?			
259	green	?	?	3
	Manufacturer: ?			
260	amber	?	?	3
	Manufacturer: ?			
261	amber	?	?	3
	Manufacturer: ?			
262	amber	B	11 1/2	3
	Manufacturer: ?			
263	amber	B	11 5/16	3
	Manufacturer: ?			
264	amber	?	?	2 1/2
	Manufacturer: ?			

	Color	Finish	Height in Inches	Diameter of Base in Inches
265	amber	B	9 3/8	2 1/2
	Manufacturer: ?			
266*	amber	B	11	2 3/4
	Manufacturer: ?			
267	amber	B	11 1/8	2 7/8
	Manufacturer: ?			
268	amber	B	11 1/2	3
	Manufacturer: ?			
269	amber	B	11 3/8	3
	Manufacturer: ?			
270*	amber	B	11 1/8	2 7/8
	Manufacturer: ?			
271	amber	A	11 1/2	3
	Manufacturer: ?			
272	green	?	?	2 7/8
	Manufacturer: ?			
273	amber	A	9 1/2	2 5/8
	Manufacturer: ?			
274	amber	B	11 7/8	3 1/8
	Manufacturer: ?			
275	amber	B	11 1/4	2 7/8
	Manufacturer: ?			
276	green	?	?	3
	Manufacturer: ?			

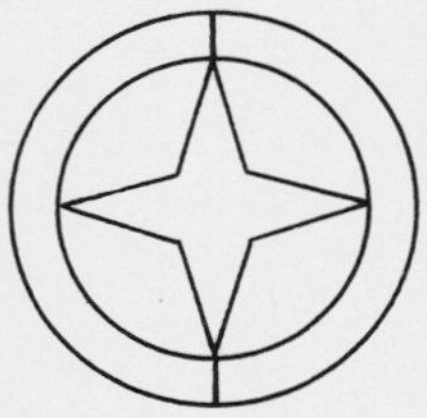

265 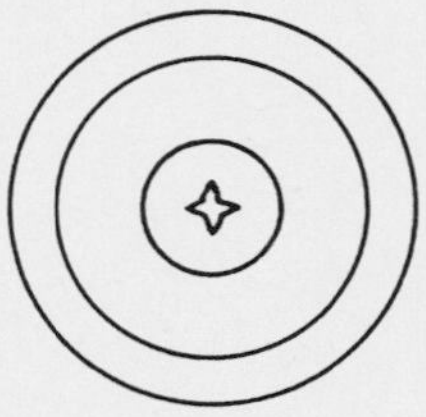 266 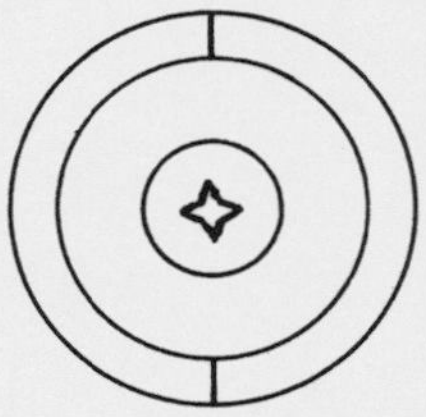 267

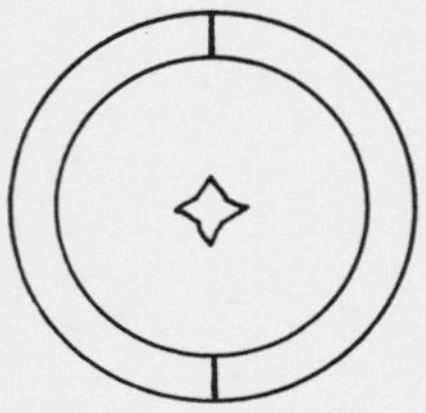

268 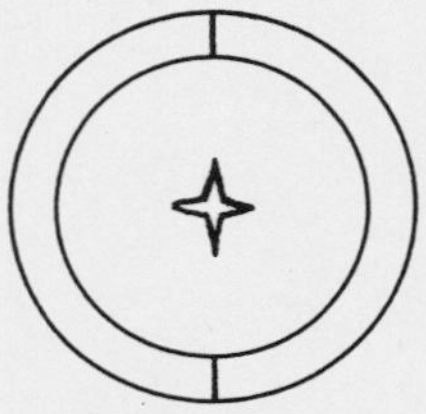 269 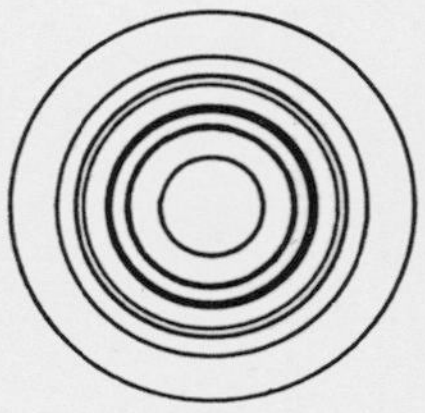 270

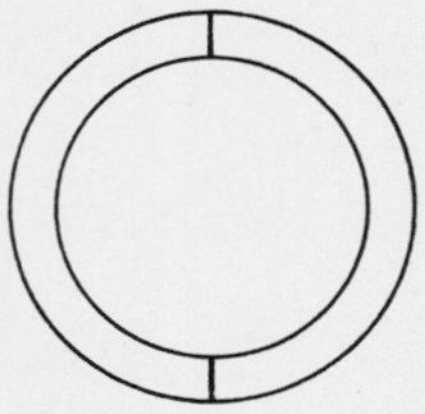

271 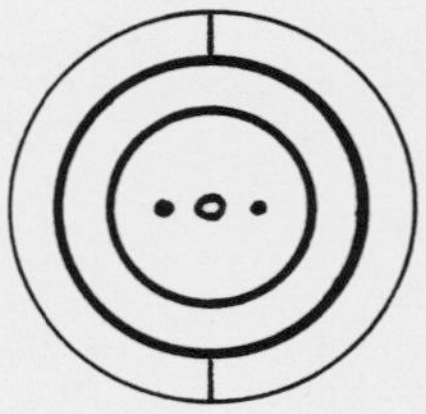 272 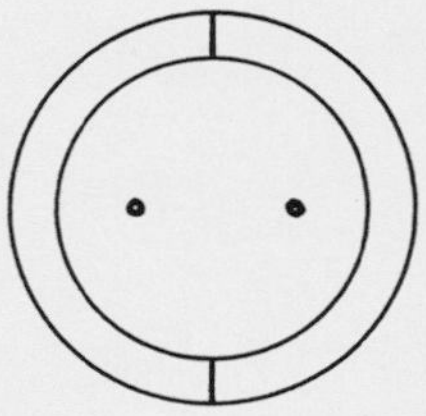 273

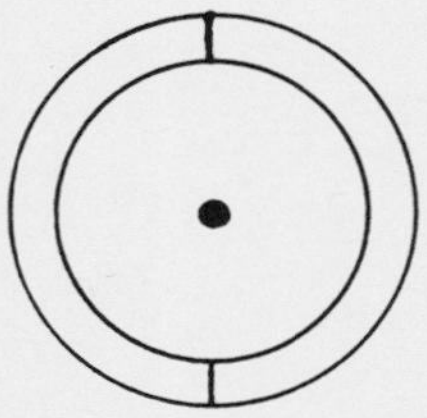

274 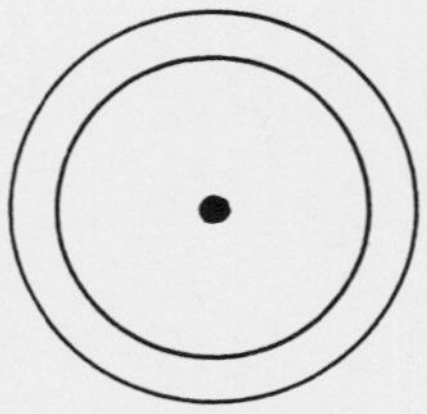 275 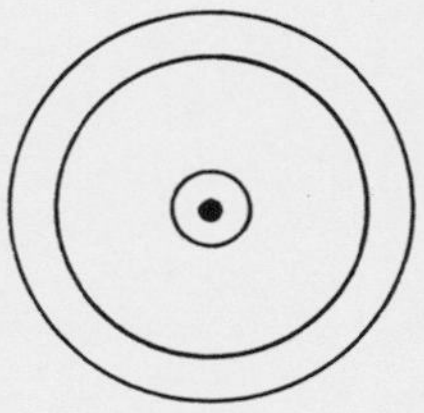 276

*Molded shoulder inscription: PATENT

APPENDIX B

A. Distribution of colors in glass beer bottles at Fort Union.*

Glass Color	Number of Types†	Percent of Total
Amber to Dark Brown	248	87
Light Blue	29	10
Dark Green	9	3
Totals	286	100

B. Distribution of colors in glass beer bottles at Fort Laramie.*

Glass Color	Number of Types†	Percent of Total
Amber to Dark Brown	174	90
Light Blue	14	7
Dark Green	2	1
Light Green	2	1
Colorless	1	1
Totals	193	100

---

* Only complete or nearly complete specimens were used in arriving at these figures; fragments of bottles were not considered.

† Type refers to a bottle that is different from another in style of neck finish and/or molded base marking.

APPENDIX C

A. Impressed Stamps on Ceramic Ale Bottles at Fort Laramie

2
MURRAY & B...
POTTERY PORTOBELLO

In 1867 a Mr. Buchan acquired a lease on a pottery formerly owned by a family named Tough, and ultimately purchased the firm. A few years later he took a partner, J. F. Murray, from the Caledonian Pottery in Glasgow. The business then became Murray and Buchan and continued so until 1877 when Murray resigned. Murray was succeeded by William Maclachlan who held a managerial position in the business for a few years until he also resigned, whereupon the pottery passed entirely into the hands of A. W. Buchan & Co. The firm was still producing large quantities of stoneware of every description as late as 1923.

H. KENNEDY
BARROWFIELD
2
POTTERY GLASGOW

Established in 1866 by Henry Kennedy, the business grew from a modest shop to one of the most extensive of the stoneware factories. Upon his death, Mr. Kennedy was succeeded by his sons Joseph and John. By 1923 the firm was operating as Henry Kennedy & Sons, Ltd.

GROSVENOR
2
GLASGOW

This firm was first known as the Bridgeton Pottery and was built in 1869 by F. Grosvenor. The pottery came to be called Eagle Pottery and the firm to be known as F. Grosvenor & Sons. It was still in operation by 1923.

B.   Impressed Stamps in Ceramic Ale Bottles at Fort Union

PORT DUNDAS
POTTERY COY.
GLASGOW

The factory was established in 1866 and made a variety of clay bottles and jars. There were several changes in ownership of the firm. Some time after 1840 the pottery was taken over by James Miller, became known as James Miller & Co., but reverted in later years to the original title "The Port Dundas Pottery Coy," by which name it was known until 1923.

RO. COOPER & CO.
PORTOBELLO

No records of this firm are known to exist.

Advertised Bottled Products: 1841–1903

The following is a compilation of bottled goods advertised in periodicals between 1841 and 1903. The intention is to provide a listing of some of the countless bottled products used in this country during the latter half of the 19th century for purposes of identification, dating, and interpretation.

Although many of the bottles listed are represented in the Fort Union and Fort Laramie collections, no attempt has been made to identify them as such. This section includes advertising only to show that a particular product was offered for sale in a certain known year and that its bottle may date from that time. Obviously, a bottle might have remained in a frontier home for many years after its purchase or after the manufacturer had gone out of business. Many products might also predate the advertisement.

The range of dates during which the products were advertised is provided in the right hand column. If an item was found to be advertised in only one year, only that year is indicated in the date column.

Sources of advertising used in the preparation of this section were the following newspapers and journals dating from 1841 to 1903:

The Argus, Albany, N.Y.	1891
Authentic World's Fair Journal (Columbian Exposition Illustrated)	1892
Boston Commonwealth	1895
The Capital	1877
The Center-Union Agriculturist	1878
Chautauqua Assembly Herald, Chautauqua, N. Y.	1892
The Chicago Times	1882–94
The Chicago Daily Tribune	1882
The Chicago Weekly Tribune	1880
Daily Chronicle, Washington	1863
Daily Covington Register	1844
Daily Critic, Washington, D.C.	1873
Daily Evening Bulletin, Philadelphia	1861–65
Daily Graphic, London	1894
The Daily Inter Ocean, Chicago	1885
Daily Leader, Bloomington, Ill.	1882
The Daily Picayune, New Orleans	1883
The Daily Richmond Enquirer	1866–67
The Denver Republican	1887
Dispatch and News, Schoolcraft, Michigan	1878
The Druggists' Journal	1876
The Earlville Phoenix, Earlville, Iowa	1894
The Easton Free Press, Penna.	1877

The Evening Express, Los Angeles	1881
The Evening Journal, Minneapolis & St. Paul	1883
Forney's Sunday Chronicle, Washington, D. C.	1877
The Glasgow Evening News, Glasgow, Scotland	1903
Harper's Bazaar	1871–72
Harper's Weekly	1857–92
The Independent, New York	1878–96
The Kansas City Journal	1903
The Licking Valley Register, Covington, Ky.	1841–44
Los Angeles Herald	1881
Meigs County Telegraph, Pomeroy, Ohio	1856–57
The Mills County Journal, Glenwood, Iowa	1876
The National Economist, Washington, D. C.	1892
The National Era, Washington, D. C.	1850–54
The New North-West, Deer Lodge City, Mont.	1869
New York Daily Tribune	1899
The New York Herald	1865
The New York Times	1873
The New York Tribune	1868
New York Weekly Tribune	1847–60
The Oberlin Herald, Oberlin, Kansas	1885

Ohio Washingtonian Organ, Cincinnati, Ohio	1846
The Philadelphia Inquirer	1865
The Prairie Farmer, Chicago	1901
Public Opinion, Washington & New York	1892
The Resources of California, San Francisco	1881
The Richmond Daily Enquirer	1869–75
The Richmond Daily Enquirer and Examiner	1869
The Richmond Daily Whig	1864–70
The Richmond Dispatch	1893–95
The Richmond Enquirer	1851–75
The Richmond Whig and Public Advertiser	1854–62
The Rocky Mountain News, Denver, Colo.	1882
The Saginaw Daily Courier, East Saginaw, Mich.	1877
Saint Paul and Minneapolis Pioneer Press	1883
The Salina Sun, Salina, Kansas	1891
Sanilac Jeffersonian, Lexington, Mich.	1876
Scranton Weekly Republican	1872
Sedalia Register, Sedalia, Mo.	1879
The Sioux City Journal, Sioux City, Iowa	1890–96
The Sioux City Journal for the Year	1892–94
Sioux City Weekly Times, Sioux City, Iowa	1875

The State Register,
Guthrie, Okla. 1901
Sunday Globe,
Pittsburgh, Pa. 1879
The Sunday Morning Free
Press, Scranton, Pa. 1879

The Times-Democrat,
New Orleans 1881–83

Uncle Sam, Manila 1898

The United Service —
A Monthly Review of
Military and Naval
Affairs, Vol. V 1881

The Virginia State Journal 1874

The Wakarusa Weekly
Sun, Wakarusa, Ind. 1876
The Washington Post 1880–94
The Washington
Weekly Post 1883

The Weekly Inter Ocean 1885
The Weekly People
of New York 1902
The Windfall News,
Windfall, Ind. 1877
Woodhull and Claflin's
Weekly, New York 1872

The Youth's Companion,
Boston 1878–88

BEER, WINE, WHISKEY

Allsop's East India
Pale Ale 1857
Alsop's Lager 1903
American Pilsener 1892
Anglo-Bavarian Pale
and Mild Ales 1894
Anheuser Beer 1892
Anheuser-Busch Beer 1893

Bass & Co's. Pale Ale 1881
Benedictine 1881
Phillip Best Brewing
Co's. Milwaukee
Export Beer 1883
Blanquefort Claret Wine 1881
Blatz Beer 1892
Booth & Sedgwick's
London Cordial Gin 1857
Budweiser Beer 1892

Cabine Champagne 1881
Cabinet Bourbon 1869
Cachet Blanc
Champagne 1881
Cambellton Scotch
Whisky 1881
Castillion & Co. Brandy 1869
Catherwood's Imperial
Cabinet Whiskey 1883
Catherwood's Imperial
Rye 1883
Catherwood's
Philadelphia
Century Whisky 1881
Catherwood's
Philadelphia
Old Stock Whisky 1881
Centennial Premium
Wine 1878–94
Champagne V. P. Fine
Cognac Brandy 1881
Clagett's Porter 1869
Clagett's Superior
Cream Ale 1869
Cook's Extra Dry
Imperial Champagne 1883–91
Cook's Imperial Wine 1891
Crow (whiskey) 1877
J. H. Cutter's O.K. No. 1
Old Bourbon Whiskey 1881

Deer Lodge Beer 1869
Dobler's Lager Beer 1891
Dog's Head Ale 1892
Dublin Distillers' Co.
Irish Whisky 1881
Duff, Gordon & Co's.
Sherry Wine 1881
Duffy's Pure Malt
Whiskey 1887–99

Eclipse Champagne 1883
George Eyssell, Druggist
(whiskey) 1903

Faust Beer 1892

Golden Wedding
(whiskey) 1877
Grape Leaf Gin 1857
Green Seal
Champagne 1881
Guinness's Extra Stout 1881
James Y. Guthrie's O.P.S.
Reindeer Whisky 1881

Hammon (whiskey) 1877
Henrich's Beer 1892
Hibbert's Porter 1862
Thomas Hine Brandy 1869

Imperial Cabinet
Whiskey 1883
Ind, Coope & Co's.
Pale Ale 1881
India Pale Ale 1894
Ives Seedling Wine 1873

Jamaica Rum 1881
St. Julian Medoc Claret
Wine 1881

Kalon Sherry 1893
Keller Bourbon 1877

Lac d'Or Champagne 1875
Lachman & Jacobi
California Wine 1881
Lemp's St. Louis Lager
Beer 1896

Mariani Wine 1894
Marrian's Pale Ale 1881
Milwaukee Beer 1881
The Christian Moerlein
Brewing Co. National
Export Lager Beer 1883
Moerlein's Cincinnati
Lager Beer 1896
Mountain Dew
(bourbon) 1854–69
Mumm's Champagne 1874

New Rochelle Blackberry
Wine 1858

O. K. (bourbon) 1869
Old Crow Rye 1899
Old Tom Gin 1881
Oporto Port Wine 1881
Overholt's Old Straight
Rye Whisky 1881

Pabst's Milwaukee Beer 1891
Perkins, Stern & Co.,
California Wines 1871
Pinet Brandy 1869

Quaker Maid Rye 1903

Reed's Celebrated London
Cordial Gin 1857
Louis Roederer Carte
Blanche Champagne 1869–81
Jules Rohn & Co.'s Cognac
Brandy 1857

Schlitz Beer (American
Bottling Co.) 1883
Schlitz Export Beer
(Voechting, Shape & Co.) 1883
Jos. Schlitz Lager Beer 1880
J. A. Shahun (bourbon) 1869
S. O. P. Cognac Brandy 1873
Speer's J. P. Brandy 1882
Speer's Port
Grape Wine 1882
Stag Brand Holland Gin 1881

G. O. Taylor Whiskies 1893

The Tip Top Beer	1883	Vins de Champagne	1873	Washington Brewery	
Trimble Whiskey	1899			Company's Lager Beer	1894
		Washington Brewery		Wolfe's Schiedam	
		Company's Capuciner	1892	Aromatic Schnapps	1854–83
United V. P. Fine Cognac		Washington Brewery			
Brandy	1881	Company's Champagne	1892		

BITTERS

Allen's Iron Tonic	1883–93	Electric	1883–92	Kelly's Old Cabin	1863
Angostura	1850–present				
Atwood's	1876	Chas. Gautier's		Malt	1880
		Native Wine	1873	Mishler's Herb	1885
Baker's Celebrated		Golden Seal	1885		
Premium	1858–70	The Great Zingari	1868	O. K. Plantation	1841
Dr. Beecher's Wild		Green's Oxygenated	1858–76	Oriental Cholera	1866
Cherry Pectoral	1873				
Boerhave's Holland	1858–76	Dr. Harter's Wild Cherry	1891	Peruvian	1871–81
Boker's	1866–91	Dr. Henley's California IXL	1881	Phenix	1858
Dr. Brady's Mandrake	1879–94	Home Stomach	1876	Plantation	1869
Browning's	1873–77	Dr. Hoofland's Celebrated		Prickly Ash	1887–91
Brown's Iron	1883–93	German	1854–76		
		Hop	1878–94	Stetler's Samaritan	1875
Dr. Clark's Sherry Wine	1858	Hops and Malt	1885	S. T. X. Plantation	1863–68
		Hostetter's	1858–1902		
Damiana	1881	Hutching's	1876	Dr. Walker's California	
Dr. J. Bovee Dod's				Vinegar	1869–76
Imperial Wine	1858	Johnson's	1876	Dr. Wistar's Old Cabinet	1870
Drake's Plantation	1868–76				

COSMETICS

Aqua De Magnolia	1866	Callopoion	1869	Famous Blush of Roses	1892
Alexandra Perfumes	1876	Mme. Caroline's Instaneous		Famous Blush of Roses	
The Andalusian Balm	1869–70	Wrinkle Remover	1892	Massage Oil	1892
Atkinson, Bazin & Taylor's		Mrs. Cobb's Cherri Lip	1886	J. Marie Farine	
Tooth Paste	1886	Mrs. Cobb's Hand Lotion	1886	Cologne	1869–71
		Mrs. Cobb's Panza Cream	1886	Floreston Cologne	1883
Balm of a Thousand		Mrs. Cobb's Zantie	1886	Fontaine's Cream	
Flowers	1857	Cold Cream	1854	of Wild Flower	1857
Barry's Tricophorous	1886	Colgate's Bandoline	1886		
Bayley's Essence Bouquet	1886	Colgate's Bay Rum	1886	Goland's Lotion	1869
Bayley's Tablets		Colgate's Glycerine Lotion	1886	Gosrell's Cherry	
Bazin's Amadine	1886	Dr. T. Feliz Courad's		Tooth Paste	1886
Bazin's Shaving Cream	1886	Oriental Cream		Gouraud's Lily White	1886
Bell's White Roses	1886	or Magical Beautifier	1892–95	Gouraud's Oriental Cream	1886
Benzoicene	1866	Courday's Cologne	1869	Dr. E. L. Graves Unequalled	
Blanc de Perle	1869	Courday's Cosmetic	1886	Tooth Powder	1892
Brille's Bay Rum	1886	Courday's Rhum		Guernsey's Balm	1858
Brown's Camphorated		and Quinine	1886		
Saponaceous Dentrifice	1888	The Crown Perfumes	1872–74	Hackmetack	1892
Burnett's Cologne	1876			Hagan's Magnolia	
Burnett's Extract		Dade's Dental Detergent	1869	Balm	1869–85
of Vanilla & Rose	1876	Day's Veloutine	1886	Hegeman's Camphor Ice	
Burnett's Florimel	1866–76	Derma Royale	1892	with Glycerine	1858–73
Burnett's Kalliston	1861–86	Dew De'Andes	1868	Humboldt's Beauty	
Burnett's Oriental		Dorin's Liquid Rouge	1886	Bouquet	1858
Tooth Wash	1866–76	Duncan's Bay Rum	1886		
Byrne's Florinda Water	1886			Indien	1886
		Eedes Extracts	1869		
Calder's Dentine	1886	Email De Paris	1865	Jacque Rose and Violet	1886

Johann M. F. Cologne	1886	Mann's Perfumes	1883	Riker's Fluid Dentrifice	1875
Jules Jared's Lemail de Paris	1867	The Marvel of Peru Perfume	1866	Rimmel's Aromatic Vinegar	1866
Kalodermine	1886	McKesson & Robbins	1876	Rimmel's Perfumes	1869–71
Kiss Me Quick Exquisite Perfume	1858	Metnedaval	1866	Ring's Ambrosia	1876
		Miller's Antheo.	1886	Roger's Fragrant Odoroline for the Teeth	1866
La Belle Balm	1894	Morris' Assorted Cachous	1876	Rowland's Macassar Oil	1869
La Belle Creme	1894	Mujaviro	1866		
La Belle Eulalia Cream	1894	Murray & Lanman's Florida Water	1870–92	Savage's Bully Vinegar	1886
La Belle Hygenic Wrinkle Annihilator	1894	Myer's Rock Rose	1876	Savage's Ursina	1867–86
La Belle Liquid Soap	1894	My Magic Wash	1858	Dr. Scott's Breath Purifier	1861
Laird's Bloom of Youth	1871–86			Societe Hygienique Oil	1886
Lait de Violette	1869	Oakley's Bay Rum	1886	Sozodont	1866–1903
Lait "Larola"	1899	Oakley's Cosmetic	1886	Sterling's Ambrosia	1876
Lavadentem	1866	Oakley's Queen Cologne	1886		
P. Le Grain's Grasse Perfumes	1894	Oakley's Toilet Waters	1886	Vaseline Pomade	1886
Lubin's Eau de Toilet	1886	Otto Rose	1854	Madame Victorine's Florentine Lotion	1871
Lubin's Extract Violette	1869–71			Vioris	1899
Ludenberg's Pastille	1886	Patey's Cold Cream	1886		
Ludenberg's Rose Powder	1886	Pearl's White Glycerine	1886	Dr. Wells Eureka	1877
Lundborg's Arcadian Pink	1871–72	Perfect Gem	1858	Wickes' Electric Oil	1871
Lundborg's Cologne	1886	Perry's Moth and Freckle Lotion	1866–86	Wright's "Alconated Blycerine Tablet"	1872
Lundborg's Lavender Water	1886	Phalon's Floral Beautifier	1868	Wright's Original Frangipanni	1857
Lundborg's Perfumes	1883–88	Phalon's Flor de Mayo	1868	Wright's Pond Lilly Toilet Wash	1880–91
Lundborg's Rhenish Cologne	1883	Phalon's Night Blooming Cereus	1866–74		
		Phalon's Paphian Lotion	1868	Mme. M. Yale's Excelsior Complexion Remedies	1894
Dr. Lyon's Tooth Paste	1873	Phalon's White Rose	1874	Mme M. Yale's Excelsior Hair Tonic	1894
		Pierre's Dentrifice	1886	Mme. M. Yale's Wrinkles and Skin Food	1894
Macy's Cologne	1886	Piesse & Lubin's Frangipanni	1858		
Macy's Toilet Waters	1886	Prepared Oil of Palm and Mace	1866	Zeno and Co.'s Highland Heather	1892
Macy's Star	1886	Price's Glycerine	1887		
Magnolia Water	1868–69	Dr. Price's Toothene	1878		
		Dr. Price's Unique Perfumes	1878		
		Queen Anne Cologne	1890		

CULINARY

Armour's Extract of Beef	1892	Horlick's Food for Infants and Invalids	1885	Dr. Price's Special Flavoring Extracts	1878–85
Atkinson's Extracts	1886			Prussing's White Wine Vinegar	1875
Blair and Wyeth's Liquid Rennet	1858	Lea & Perrin's Sauce	1858–90		
Burnett's Celebrated Flavoring Extracts	1863–83	Lundborg's Extracts	1886	Roe & Co's Salad Oil	1886
		Macy's Extracts	1886	Rowat's Pure Grape Vinegar	1903
California Catsup or Golden Sauce	1871	Mann's Flavoring Extracts	1883	Rowat's Tomato Catsup	1903
Careme's Anglo-French Sauce	1866–67	Morris' Concentrated Extracts	1876		
Coleman's Mustard	1869	Morris' Double Extracts	1876	Thomas' Flavoring Extracts	1876
Comstock's Rational Food	1869–76			Turner's Raspberry Syrup	1858
		Nestle's Lacteous Farina	1871–73		
		Norton's Jockey Club Sauce	1868	Viconti's Tuscan Salad Oil	1873
Halford Leicestershire Table Sauce	1871–73	Oakley's Extracts	1886	Lord Ward's Worcestershire Sauce	1858
Hecker's Farina	1868	Olden's Pure Concentrated Fruit Jelly	1872	Wood's Pure Flavoring Extracts	1884

HAIR AND BEARD PREPARATIONS

Aaragon Hair Restorer	1879		Frizzine	1892		Parker's Hair Balsam	1883–95
Mrs. S. A. Allen's World's						Pearson & Co.'s Circassian	
Hair Restorer	1857–87		Gilman's Hair Dye	1854		Hair Rejuvenator	1866
Apiastrum	1875		Golden Unguent	1874		Pestachine	1866
Ayers Hair Vigor	1875–1903		Golden O'Dor	1866		Pinaud's Brilliantine	1886
						Phalon Hair Invigorator	1874
Balsam of the Tennessee			Hair Grower	1877		Phalon's Vitalia	1870
Swamp Shrub	1866		Hair Revivum	1880			
Balsam Flowers	1857		Hall's Vegetable Sicillian			Reparator Capilli	1867
Bandoline	1886		Hair Renewer	1867–91		Riley's Beautifier	1868
Barney's Cocoa Castorine	1858		Heimstreet's Hair Coloring	1876		Robares' Aueroline	1886
Barry's Safe Hair Dye	1871		Herpicide	1903		Prof. Robb's Curlique	1866
Barry's Tricopherous	1858–88		Hiawatha Hair Dye	1869		Russell's Italian	
Batchelor's Celebrated			Hill's Instantaneous			Compound	1866
Hair Dye	1854–78		Hair Dye	1869–76		Russian Hair Dye	1876
Bazin's Amandine	1854–86		Hoosier Curling Fluid	1892			
Bazin's Shaving Cream	1886					Dr. Sevign's Restrarateur	
Blair's Richmond			Imperial Hair Regenerator	1899		Capillaire	1866–67
Hair Dye	1867–76					Shilling Hair Tonic	1858
Bogle's Hyperion Fluid	1849–57		Mrs. Jackson's Hair			Dr. Sterling's Ambrosia	1863
Brilles' Bay Rum	1886		Restorer	1867		Stewart's Celebrated	
Buckingham's			Dr. Jayne's Hair Tonic	1842–70		Dandruff Eradicator and	
Whisker Dye	1876–83		Henry Johnson's Genuine			Hair Restorative	1846
Burnett's Cocoaine	1858–88		Bear's Oil	1847			
Prof. Butler's Magnetic			John A. Jones National			Thompson's Pomade	
Curlique	1868		Hair Dye	1854		Optime	1875
			Jules Hauel's Eau Athenienne				
Carboline	1881		Hair Renovator	1861		Upham's Hair Gloss	1876
Chevalier's Life							
for the Hair	1868–87		Dr. Kennedy's Hair Tea	1871–72		Ezekiel's Virginia	
Circassian Hair						Hair Restorer	1867
Restorative	1876		London Hair Color				
Cosmoline Pomade	1875		Restorer	1866		Ward's Walnut Oil	1892
Courday's Pomade	1886		Louden's Oriental			Webster's Vegetable Hair	
Cristadoro's Excelsior			Hair Tonic	1876		Invigorator	1866
Hair Dye	1857–76		Lyon's Kathairon	1854–69		West India Bay Rum	1854
Cristadoro's Hair						Mrs. Wilson's Hair	
Preservative	1870		Mansfield's Capillaries	1884		Dressing	1861
Curlica	1874		Massacoit Hair Restorer			Mrs. Wilson's Hair	
			and Dressing	1876		Regenerator	1861
Prof. DeBreux's Frisier			Matthew's Hair Dye	1876		Woodland Cream	1857
Le Cheveux	1866–67		Mayor's Walnut Oil	1903		Prof. Wood's Hair	
Delluc's Eau Angelizue	1886		L. Miller's Hair			Restorative	1856–58
Denslow's Hair Tonic	1861		Invigorator	1858		Wood's Improved Hair	
Depellerine	1873		Morse's Revivum	1876		Restorative	1876
Dykes Beard Elixir	1875		Mott's Chemical Pomade	1866			
						Yucca	1890
Eureka Hair Dye	1866		Oakley's Bay Rum	1886		Zoecome	1872

INK AND GLUE

Arnold's Copying Ink	1876		Kirk's Fine Premium			The Shilling Indelible Ink	1861
Arnold's Writing Fluid	1876		Mucilage	1894		Spalding's Prepared	
						Glue	1858–83
Carmine, Conger and			Lanz's Magic Ink	1866		Stafford's Ink	1876
Field's	1876						
Carmine, Gulott's	1876		Maynard and Noyes' Ink	1876		R. Titcomb's Premium	
Coaquline Diamond			Muchmore's Glue Pot	1876		Writing Ink	1846
Cement	1870					Twin Bottle Ink Eraser	1885
Conger and Field			Payson's Indelible Ink	1876			
Writing Fluid	1858		Pearl Mucilage	1888		Van Stan's Stratena	1878
David's Ink	1876		Peerless Ink	1876			
			Peerless Mucilage	1876		Worden and Hyatt's	
Kirk's Fine Premium			Proctor's Liquid Glue	1885		Violet Inks	1876
Black Ink	1894						

MEDICATED WATERS

Alleghany	1869	Hathorne	1883	Ottawa Natural	
Apenta	1899–93	Hawthorne Water	1877	Mineral Water	1885
Appolinaris	1885	High Rock	1885		
		Hub Punch	1881	Rockbridge Alum	1869
Bath Healing Water	1869	Hungarian Aperient		Ruszti Asszu	1892
Bethesda Spring Water	1873	Water	1887		
Blue Lick	1877	Hunyadi János	1885	Sanicula	1885
Buffalo Lithia Water	1888–91			Saratoga Geyser	
				Spring Water	1872–85
Congress Water	1858–77	Londonerry Lithia Water	1891	Seltzer Water	1877
Crab Orchard	1893			Silurian	1885
		Magnolia Water	1868	Star	1885
Empire Water	1877	Manitou Water	1887–92	St. Leon	1877
		Mear Lithia Water	1887		
Friedrichshall Bitter Water	1877	Me'nesi Asszu	1892	Vermont Spring Water	1868
		Missispuoi Water	1876	Vichy (St. Elizabeth,	
				St. Mary, Tracy)	1869–99
Gettysburg Katalysine	1868–73				
Geyser Water	1877	David Nicholson's		White Sulphur	
Greenbrier White Sulphur	1869	Liquid Bread	1893	Spring Water	1871–76

MISCELLANEOUS

Denslow's Purified and		Genuine Silver Fluid	1873	0. Jouven's Inodorous Kid	
Concentrated Benzine	1861	Glenfield Patent Starch	1857	Glove Cleaner	1875
		London Paint Oil	1857		
French Dressing		Frank Miller's Water-Proof		Pratt's Astral Oil	1873
(shoe dressing)	1878	Oil Blacking	1868	0. Shilling Benzine	1858

PATENT MEDICAL PREPARATIONS

Ale and Beef "Peptonized"	1892	Ballard's Horehound		Brou	1894
Allen's Brain Food	1883	Syrup	1894–93	Brou's Injection	1891
Allen's Lung Balsam	1870–82	Ballard's Snow		Brown's Bronchial	
The American Remedy	1885	Liniment	1894–93	Troches	1885–88
Ammoniated Cough		Baker's Pain Panacea	1876–93	Brown's Chlordyne	1871–76
Mixture	1892	Barry's Tricopherous	1876–93	Brown's Essence of	
Anodyne Liniment	1875	Bartholie's Mothers'		Jamaica Ginger	1879–95
Arabian Liniment	1870	Relief	1876–93	Brown's Jamaica Ginger	1876
Arend's Beef, Iron, and Wine,		Bateman's Drops	1876–93	Brown's Teething	
with Cinchona	1882	Bell of Bourbon	1887–93	Cordial	1879–94
Arend's Kumyss	1882	Big G	1887–91	Bruiere's Invigorant	1868
Arnold's C. Killer	1876	Bininger's Old London		Bubier's Laxative Salz	1895
Dr. Seth Arnold's Balsam	1866	Dock Gin	1858–68	Buchupaiba	1882–83
Aroud's Ferruginous		Biokrene	1876	Dr. Bull's Cough Syrup	1883–92
Wine	1883	Bishop Soule's Liniment	1876	Burbank's Elixir Opium	1876
Atherton's Wild		Blackberry Balsam	1883	Burbank's Seltzer Aperient	1876
Cherry Syrup	1876	Blood Food	1858	Burdsall's Arnica Liniment	1858
Athlophoras	1884–85	Boericke and Tafel	1882–93	Burnett's Cod Liver Oil	1869
Aubergier's		Dr. Bosanko's Cough		Butler's Balsamic Mixture	
Lactucarius	1892	and Lung Syrup	1883–93	of Cubebs and Copabia	1871
August Flower	1891	Botanic Blood Balm	1893	Butt's Bromo Lithis	1893
Ayer's Ague Cure	1867–83	Bradfield's Female			
Ayer's Cherry Pectoral	1854–99	Regulator	1892	California Syrup of Figs	1887–93
Ayer's Pills	1876	Bradford's Pink Bottle	1876	Calthos	1892
Ayer's Sarsaparilla	1858–94	Dr. Brandreth's External		Carter's Little Liver Pills	1893–96
		Remedy or Liniment	1842	Carter's Spanish Mixture	1854–56
B. T. Babbitt's		Bristol's Sarsaparilla	1848	Case's Compound	
Best Saleratus	1857–93	British Oil	1876	Syrup of Tar	1872

Castoria	1876–93
Caswell, Hazard & Co.'s Pure Cod Liver Oil	1883
Centaur Liniment	1873–83
Chamberlain's Colic, Cholera & Diarrhoea Remedy	1892–96
Chamberlain's Pain Balm	1894
Chamberlain's Remedy	1894
Dr. Charles's European Cholera Remedy	1866
Charles's London Cordial Gin	1858–76
Cheeseman's Arabian Balsam	1876
Cheeseman's Female Pills	1876
Cherokee Cure	1876
Cherokee Injection	1876
Cherokee Pills	1876
Cherokee Remedy	1876
Chichester's Dyspepsia Specific	1857
Dr. Churchill's Remedy for Consumption	1858
Sir James Clarke's Celebrated Female Pills	1856
Clove Anodyne Toothache Drops	1858–61
Coca Cola	1891–92
Cockle's Pills	1876
Coe's Cough Balsam	1866–76
Coe's Dyspepsia Cure	1866–76
Colicura	1883
Compound of Hypophosphites	1858
Compound Oxygen	1881
Compound Syrup of Sarsaparilla	1843–44
Compound Tincture Opium	1867
Condurango	1872–73
Constitution Life Syrup	1866–68
Constitution Water	1861–76
Cook's Syrup of Bark	1869
Sir Astley Cooper's Vital Restorative	1881–83
Corbin's Worm Syrup	1876
Cordial Balm of Syricum—Tonic Pills	1875
Rev. I. Covert's Balm of Life	1842
Dr. Cox's Vermifuge and Tincture	1846
Dr. Cram's Fluid Lightning	1876
Crossman's Specific Mixture	1894
Crystal Eyedrops	1858
Culp Salvation Oil	1892
Cuticura Resolvent	1882–92
Dade's Corn Killer	1869
Dalley's Magical Pain Extractor	1866
Carby's Prophylactic Fluid	1882
Perry Davis Pain Killer	1840–91

DeBrath's Electric Oil	1858–76
Deem's Hepatic Pills	1876
Dr. De Jongh's Light-Brown Cod Liver Oil	1875–76
Delamarre's Specific Pills	1876
DeWitt's Little Early Risers	1892
D. I. C.	1881
Digestive Pepsine Elixix	1883
Disbrow's Anisette Cordial	1870
Double Chlorida of Gold	1885
Dove's Compound Fluid Extract of Cissampelos Pareira	1870–71
Rev. N. H. Downs Vegetable Elixir	1858–78
DuBarry's Revalenta Arab. F'd.	1876
Dulby's Carminative	1870
Dr. Duncan's Expectorant Remedy for Consumption	1842
Dupuy's Bilious Corrective	1858
Durang's Rheumatic Remedy	1877
Duval & Norton's Celebrated Horse Tonic	1871
Eilert's Extract of Tar and Wild Cherry	1876
Electro Silicon	1876
Elias' Effectual Eradicator	1869
Elias's Conglutine	1870
Elixir Babek	1890–93
Elixir of J. F. Bernard of Paris	1872
Ely's Cream Balm	1885–90
Epileptic Remedy	1891
Euca-Lyptus Cordial	1890
Eureka	1858
Extract of Cannabus Indica	1857
Fahnestock's Liniment	1843–44
B. A. Fahnestock's Vermifuge	1848–76
Dr. Faton's Infantile Cordial	1858
Dr. Fenner's Blood and Liver Remedy & Nerve Tonic	1879
Dr. Fenner's Golden Relief	1879
Dr. Fenner's Improved Cough Honey	1879
Dr. Fenner's St. Vitas Dance Specific	1879
Fellows' Compound Syrup of Hypophosphites	1880
Ferro-Phosphorated Elixir of Calisaya	1869–83
Finney's Compound Elixir of Buchu	1880
Dr. Fitler's Great Vegetable Rheumatic Remedy	1868

Fleury's Wa-Hoo Tonic	1882
Food Cure	1878
B. Fosgatt's Anodyne Cordial	1858
Foss's Compound Extract of Yellow Dock and Sarsaparilla	1848
Fougera's Iodinized Cod Liver Oil	1869
Fowle's Pile and Humor Cure	1872–75
French Specific	1885
"G"	1883
Gardiner's Rheumatic and Neuralgia Compound	1861
Mrs. M. N. Gardner's Indian Balsam of Liverwort	1858
Gardner's Pimple Destroyer	1858
Dr. E. F. Garvin's Solution and Compound Elixir of Tar	1872
Gastron	1877
Gaudichaud's Extract of Sandal Wood	1876
German Syrup	1891
Giles Liniment Iodide Ammonia	1879–94
Glen Flora Water	1875
Godfrey's Catarrh Remedy	1866
Godfrey's Cordial	1876
Dr. Goldenberg's Kidney & Liver Specific	1877
Dr. Goldenberg's Remedies	1877
Goodale's Errhine	1857
The Graofenberg Vegetable Pills	1866
Grant's Remedy	1878
Gray's Specific Medicine	1883
Dr. Grove's Liquid Catarrh Remedy	1858
The Great English Remedy	1878–82
The Great German Remedy	1858
Dr. Green's Nervura Blood and Nerve Remedy	1893–94
Gregory's Bilious Pills	1876
Gregory's Extract Opium	1876
Gridley's Salt Theum Ointment	1844
Grimault and Co.'s Brazilian Guarana	1867
Grimault and Co.'s Ferruginous Peruvian Bark Wine with Malaga	1883
Grimault and Co.'s Liquid Extract of Matico Vegetalis	1867
Grimault and Co.'s Syrup of Hypophosphite of Lime	1867

Grimault and Co.'s Syrup of Iodized Horse Radish	1867
Dr. Grupott's Yellow Dock and Sarsaparilla	1882
Haemar	1877
Dr. Haines' Golden Specific	1892
Dr. Hale's Family Medicine	1879
Hale's Honey of Horehound and Tar	1876–86
Dr. Wm. Hall's Balsam for the Lungs	1866–96
Hall's Catarrh Cure	1891–95
Dr. Halliday's Blood Purifier	1883
Dr. Hart's Vegetable Extract	1847–49
Dr. Harter's Iron Tonic	1882–83
Hasting's Compound Syrup of Naptha	1847–48
Hatch's Universal Cough Syrup	1877
Hawley's (Liebigs) Food	1875
Hawley's Saccherated Pepsin	1875
Hawley's Wine Pepsin	1875
Hazard and Caswell's Cod Liver Oil	1868–76
Hegeman Clark & Co.'s Genuine Cod Liver Oil	1858
Hegeman's Cod Elix. Calya.	1876
Hegeman's Cod Liver Oil	1869–76
Hegeman's Ferrated Elixir of Bark	1869
Helmbold's Bushu	1876
Helmbold's Compound Fluid Extract	1856
Helmbold's Compound Fluid Extract Buchu	1856–71
Helmbold's Genuine Preparation	1856–68
Helmbold's Improved Rose Wash	1866–76
Helmbold's Pills	1876
Helmbold's Sarsaparilla	1866–76
Prof. Henderson's Golden Ambrosia	1892
Henry's Calcinated Magnesia	1888
Hepatic Elixir	1842
Dr. Herring's Veronica Lung Extract	1876
Heymann's Dyspepsia Elixir	1854
Hibbard's Circassian Balm	1876
Rev. B. Hibbard's Pills	1876
Hill's Balsam of Honey	1876
Hoff's Malt Extract	1894
Holloway's Pills	1866
Hood's Sarsaparilla	1883–96
Horsford's Acid Phosphate	1873–95

Howe's Never-Failing Ague Cure & Tonic Bitters	1878
Humphrey's Homeopathic Specific	1893
Humphrey's Veterinary Cure Oil	1893
Huntington's Cascarilla	1876
Hunt's Remedy	1883
Hyatt's 'A B' Double Strength Balsam	1876
Hyatt's Infallible Life Balsam	1876
Hyatt's Inza	1876
Hyatt's Pulmonic Life Balsam	1876
Hyatt's Swiss Liniment	1876
Hydrate of Chloral	1870
Injection Malydor	1894
Iodide of Ammonia	1874
Dr. Jackson's Compound Syrup of Sassafras and Wild Cherry	1843–44
James' Celebrated Liniment	1866
Dr. H. James Extract of Cannabus Indica	1857–60
Jayne's Ague Mixture	1881
Jayne's Alterative	1870–81
Dr. Jayne's Carminative Balsam	1842–81
Dr. Jayne's Expectorant	1842–91
Jayne's Liniment or Counter Irritant	1881
Jayne's Pills	1876
Jayne's Sanative Pills	1881
Jayne's Specific	1881
Dr. Jayne's Tonic Vermifuge	1842
Jeffries Antidote	1876
Johnson's Fluid Beef	1885
Johnson's Rheumatic Compound	1876
Johnson's Toothache Drops	1847
Dr. Clark Johnson's Indian Blood Syrup	1879–94
Karle's Clover Root	1894
Karsner's Catarrh Treatment	1876
Kearney's Fluid Extract Buchu	1877
Kellinger's Infallible Liniment	1876
Kemp's Balsam	1891
Kennedy's Discovery	1876–91
Kennedy's Favorite Remedy	1885–93
Kennedy's Scrofula Ointment	1868
Kidney Wort	1880–85
King of the Blood	1881
Dr. King's New Discovery for Consumption	1892–94

King's Prepared Prescription	1876
Dr. Kline's Great Nerve Restorer	1891
Dr. Kirby's Cholera Drops	1849
Kitchel's Liniment	1865
Kitchel's Spavin Cure	1865
Knight's King of Pain	1876
Koskoo	1870
Kunkel's Bitter Wine of Iron, E. F.	1879
E. F. Kunkel's Worm Syrup	1879
Dr. La Mar's Seminal Pills	1881
Laville's Liquor	1881
Dr. Leathe's Yellow Dock Syrup	1858–60
Dr. Peter H. Lee's Asthma Medicine	1848
Dr. Leras's Phosphate of Iron	1867–83
Liebig's Company's Coca Beef Tonic	1883
Liebig's Extract of Meat	1869–96
Lindsey's Blood Searcher	1878–82
Liquid Ozone	1876
Little's White Oil	1866–70
Louden's Alterative	1876
Louden's Carminative Balsam	1876
Louden's Cherokee Liniment	1876
Louden's Female Elixir	1876
Louden's Fever and Ague Pills	1876
Louden's Indian Expectorant	1876
Louden's Pile Remedy	1876
Louden's Sanative Pills	1876
Louden's Tonic Vermifuge	1876
Lyon's Per. Drops	1876
Dr. McLane's Celebrated Vermifuge	1854–76
Dr. C. McLane's Celebrated American Worm Specific or Vermifuge	1876–78
Dr. C. McLane's Vermifuge	1883
Dr. Jas. McClintock's Family Medicines	1858–60
Dr. Maniotta's East India Tonic	1847
Dr. J. B. Marchisi's Celebrated Uterine Catholicon	1858–60
Dr. Mariotte's Infallible Toothache Remedy	1858–60
Marsden's Carminative Syrup	1866
Marshall's Uterine Catholicon	1858–66

Martin's Extract Jamaica Ginger	1876
Dr. Martin's Family Medicines	1842
Dr. Martin's Never Failing Vegetable Worm Destroying Medicine for Children	1842
Massta's Balsam	1876
Mathey Caylus' Capsules	1883
Mensman's Peptonized Beef Tonic	1878
Merchant's Gargling Oil	1870
Mexican Mustang Liniment	1852–85
Dr. Miles Nervine	1891–92
Dr. Miles New Heart Cure	1892
Dr. Mintie's Kidney Remedy . . . . .phreticum	1881
Moffat's Celebrated Medicines	1842
Moore's Ague Cure	1867
Morrison's Pills	1876
Morse's Invigorating Cordial	1876
Mother's Friend	1892–94
Dr. Mott's Balsamic Cough Syrup	1848
Mott's Headache Cure	1873–74
Mott's Vege. Liver Pills	1876
Dr. Mozley's Lemon Elicit	1890
Munyon's Homeopathic Remedies	1894
Murdock's Liquid Food	1885
Murray's Fld. Magnesia	1876
Muscovitus Tooth Ache Drops	1842
National Colic Remedy	1885
National Foot Dressing	1885
National Grease Heel Lotion	1885
National Liniment	1885
Nerve and Brain Salt	1894
Nichol's Elixir Bark & Iron	1876
Nichol's Iron Tonic	1885
Nolandine	1869
Norton's C. Pills	1876
Norton's New Remedy for Catarrh	1866
Norton's Ointment	1873
Norwegian Balm	1878
Norwood's Tincture	1876
Nowill's Pect. Honey of Liverwort	1876
O. & C.'s Colic, Cholera and Diarrhoea Remedy	1876
One Minute Cough Cure	1892–94
Opodeldoc Liquid	1876
Osborne's Nerve & Bone Liniment	1876
Osborne's Ointment	1876
Osgood's Cholagogue	1876
Dr. Osgood's India Cholagogue	1846
Otitine	1866

P. P. P.	1893
Pabst's Okay Specific	1892
Paine's Celery Compound	1887
Paine's True Chloral Soother	1870
Park's Balsam Wild Cherry	1876
Parker's Ginger Tonic	1883–95
Parker's Pleasant Worm Syrup	1885
Parker's Tonic	1885
Perry's Dead Shot Vermifuge	1895
Perry's Improved Comedone & Pimple Remedy	1872–75
Peruvian Syrup	1858–77
Peruvian Syrup and Iron Tonic	1875
Pettit's Canker Balsam	1876
Dr. Pierce's Alt. Ext.	1873–75
Dr. Pierce's Catarrh Remedy	1881
Dr. Pierce's Compound Extract of Smart Weed	1875–85
Dr. Pierce's Favorite Prescription	1875–92
Dr. Pierce's Golden Medical Discovery	1874–94
Dr. Pierce's Pleasant Purgative Pellets	1875–94
Pike's Toothache Drops	1882
Pilon	1877
Lydia E. Pinkham's Liver Pills	1883
Lydia E. Pinkham's Vegetable Compound	1883–96
Piso's Cure for Consumption	1888–96
Piso's Remedy for Catarrh	1891–92
Pitcher's Castoria	1880–81
Planten's Castor Oil, Turpentine, etc.	1876
Pond's Extract Witch Hazel	1876
Pond's Extract	1878–92
Dr. Post's Rheumatic Remedy	1868
Powers' Syrup of Tolu and Wild Cherry	1870
Pratt's Abolition Oil	1881
Dr. Price's Extract Jamaica Ginger	1878
Dr. Price's Golden Medical Discovery	1890–93
Price's Sovereign Cure	1868
Proctor's Cod Liver Oil	1876
Queru's Cod Liver Oil Jelly	1876
Quinn-Laroche	1882–96
Radway's Ready Relief	1854–99
Dr. Radway's Sarsaparillian Resolvent	1854–85

Ransom's Hive Syrup and Tolu Throat and Lung Remedies	1858–60
Read's Syrup of Liverwort	1876
Red Seal Sarsaparilla	1893
Reed's East India Remedies	1878
Reed's Throat and Lung Balsam	1858–60
Regan's Liniment	1879–94
Renne's Magic Oil	1876
Rennold's Pills	1869
Rex Brand Extract of Beef	1896
Reynold's Gout Specific	1876
Dr. Richau's Golden Balsam No. 1	1869
Dr. Richau's Golden Balsam No. 2	1869
Dr. Richau's Golden Antidote	1869
Dr. Richau's Elixir d'Amour	1869
Ring's Rose Injection	1876
Roake's Iodine Liniment	1847
Dr. Roback's Scandinavian Remedies	1856–57
Dr. Roban's Rheumatic Cure	1858–60
Dr. Robertson's Elixir of Health	1861
Dr. Robertson's Gout and Rheumatic Drops	1861
Dr. Robertson's Vegetable Nervous Cordial	1861
Roche's Embrocation	1876
Roger's Citrate of Magnesia	1878
Roger's Indian Fever Cure	1876
Roger's Liverwort and Tar	1876
Roger's Royal Nervine	1890
Rogers & Co.'s Cod Liver Oil	1876
Dr. Roger's Syrup of Liverwort and Tar	1846
Roman Eye Balsam	1847–61
Roof's Ringbone Cure	1876
Rook's Good Samaritan	1862
Dr. H. G. Root's Remedy	1887
Ross Epileptic Remedies	1874
Ruston's Cod Liver Oil	1858–60
Dr. Sage's Catarrh Remedy	1874–94
St. Jacobs' Oil	1882–91
Sal-Muscatelle	1885
Salvation Oil	1892–95
Samaritan Nervine	1883
Samaritan's Root & Herb Juices	1868
Dr. Sanborn's Liquid Catarrh Remedy	1858–60
Sand's Sarsaparilla	1843–76
Sanford's Liver Invigorator	1869–77

SELECTED READINGS

1. Bottles: General References (19th century)

Colcleaser, Donald E.
  1965 *Bottles of Bygone Days, Part I*. Betty's Letter Shop: Vallejo, California.

  1966 *Bottles of Bygone Days; Part II*. Betty's Letter Shop: Vallejo, California.

Davis, Martin and Helen Davis
  1967 *Antique Bottles*. Gandee Printing Center: Medford, Oregon.

Eastin, June
  1965 *Bottles West*. Volume 1. Press-tige: Ontario, California.

Ferraro, Pat and Bob Ferraro
  1966 *A Bottle Collector's Book*. Western Printing and Publishing Co.: Sparks, Nevada.

Freeman, Larry
  1964 *Grand Old American Bottle*. Watkins Glen, New York.

Jones, May
  1962–1968 *The Bottle Trail*. Volumes 1–9. May Jones: Nara Visa, New Mexico.

Kendrick, Grace
  1963 *The Antique Bottle Collector*. Western Printing and Publishing Co.: Sparks, Nevada.

Lorrain, Dessamae
  1968 "An Archaeologist's Guide to Nineteenth Century American Glass." *Historical Archaeology* 2: 35–44.

Lyons, Bill and Jean Lyons
  1967 *Bottles from Bygone Days*. Beeyay Publishers: South Vienna, Ohio.

McKearin, George and Helen McKearin
  1968 *American Glass*. Crown Publishers: New York.

Munsey, Cecil
  1970 *The Illustrated Guide to Collecting Bottles*. Hawthorne Books Inc.: New York.

Newman, T. Stell
  1970 "A Dating Key for Post-Eighteenth Century Bottles." *Historical Archaeology* 4: 70–75.

Putnam, H. E.
  1965 *Bottle Identification*. Published by the Author: Jamestown, California.

Switzer, Ronald R.
  1974 *The Bertrand Bottles: A Study of 19th-Century Glass and Ceramic Containers*. National Park Service, U.S. Department of the Interior, Washington, D. C.

Talbot, Olive
  1974 "The Evolution of Glass Bottles for Carbonated Drinks." *Post-Medieval Archaeology* 8. London.

Toulouse, Julian Harrison
  1971 *Bottle Makers and Their Marks*. Thomas Nelson Inc. Camden.

Tufts, James W.
  1969 *The Manufacture and Bottling of Carbonated Beverages,
  Including Sodas, Mineral Waters, Bitters, Cordials, Cham-
  pagnes, Tonics, Gingers, Ales, etc.* Frontier Book Co.:
  Fort Davis.

Van Rennsselaer, Stephen
  1969 *Early American Bottles and Flasks* Revised edition ed. by
  J. Edmund Edwards: Stratford.

White, John R.
  1978 "Bottle Nomenclature: a Glossary of Landmark Terminology
  for the Archaeologist." *Historical Archaeology* 12: 58–77.

Wilson, Rex
  1959 "Evidence in Empty Bottles." *El Palacio* 66(4): 120–123.
  1961 "A Classification System for 19th Century Bottles."
  Arizoniana 2(4): 2–6.

Yount, John T.
  1967 *Bottle Collector's Handbook and Pricing Guide.* Action
  Printery: San Angelo, Texas.

2. Histories of Fort Union and Fort Laramie

Crocchiola, Stanley Francis Louis
  1953 *Fort Union, New Mexico.*

Ehrenhard, John E.
  1972 "The Rustic Hotel: Fort Laramie National Historic Site." MS
  on file Midwest Archaeological Center, Lincoln, Nebraska.

  1973 "The Rustic Hotel, Fort Laramie National Historic Site,
  Wyoming." *Historical Archaeology* 7: 11–29.

Emmet, Chris
  1965 *Fort Union and the Winning of the Southwest.* University of
  Oklahoma Press: Norman.

Falk, Carl R.
  1971 "Archaeological Investigations at Fort Laramie, National
  Historic Site, 1971: An Interim Report." MS on file at the Midwest
  Archaeological Center, Lincoln, Nebraska.

Husted, Wilfred M.
  1964 "Archaeological Test Excavations at Fort Laramie National
  Historic Site, Wyoming, 1963." U.S. National Park Service,
  Midwest Archaeological Center, Lincoln, Nebraska.

Mattes, Merrill J.
  1969 *The Great Platte River Road: the Covered Wagon Mainline
  via Fort Kearny to Fort Laramie.* Nebraska State Historical
  Society: Lincoln.

Murray, Robert A.
  1969 *Fort Laramie: Visions of a Grand Old Post.* Old Army Press:
  Fort Collins, Colorado.

Nadeau, Remi A.
  1967 *Fort Laramie and the Sioux Indians.* Prentice Hall: Engle-
  wood Cliffs, New Jersey.

U.S. National Park Service
  1966 *Fort Union National Monument, New Mexico.* National Park
  Service, United States Department of the Interior: Washington,
  D.C.

Utley, Robert Marshall
 1953 *Fort Union in Miniature.* Stagecoach Press: Santa Fe, New Mexico.
 1962 *Fort Union National Monument, New Mexico.* United States Department of the Interior, National Park Service: Washington, D.C.

Wilson, Rex L.
 1961 "Clay Tobacco Pipes From Fort Laramie." *Annals of Wyoming* 33(2) October. Wyoming State Historical Society, Cheyenne.
 1965 "Archaeology and Everyday Life at Fort Union, New Mexico." *New Mexico Historical Review* 40(1): 55–64. University of New Mexico Press: Albuquerque.
 1966 "Tobacco Pipes From Fort Union, New Mexico." *El Palacio* 73(1): 32–40. Museum of New Mexico: Santa Fe.
 1971 *Clay Tobacco Pipes From Fort Laramie National Historic Site and Related Locations.* Office of Archaeology and Historic Preservation, National Park Service, Department of the Interior: Washington, D.C.

3. Specific Bottle Types and Related Topics

Abel, Bob
 1976 *The Book of Beer.* Regnevy: Chicago.

Baron, Stanley
 1962 *Brewed in America: a History of Beer and Ale in the United States.* Little, Brown and Co.: Boston.
Carson, Gerald
 1963 *The Social History of Bourbon, an Unhurried Account of our Star-Spangled American Drink.* Dodd-Mead: New York.

Cooper, Isabella Mitchell
 1937 *References Ancient and Modern to the Literature on Beer and Ale.* United Brewers Industrial Foundation: New York.

Crowgey, Henry G.
 1971 *Kentucky Bourbon: The Early Years of Whiskey Making.* University of Kentucky Press: Lexington.

Devner, Kay
 1968 *Patent Medicine Picture.* Privately printed by the author: Tucson.

Fountain, John C. and Donald E. Colcleaser
 1968 *Dictionary of Soda and Mineral Water Bottles.* Ole Empty Bottle House Publishing Co.: Amador City, California.

Krebs, Roland
 1953 *Making Friends is Our Business, 100 Years of Anheuser-Busch.* St. Louis.

McKearin, Helen and Kenneth M. Wilson
 1978 *American Bottles and Flasks and Their Ancestry.* Crown Publishers: New York.

Persons, Warren Milton
 1938 *Beer and Brewing in America: An Economic Study.* United Brewers Industrial Foundation, Revised by Standard Statistics Co., Inc.: New York.

Thoman, Gallus
 1909 *American Beer: Glimpses of its History and Description of its Manufacture.* United States Brewers Association: New York.

Thompson, James H.
   1947 *Bitters Bottles*. Century House: Watkins Glen: New York.

Toulouse, Julian Harrison
   1969 *Fruit Jars: A Collector's Manual*. Everybody's Press:
      Hanover, Pa.

Watson, Richard
   1965 *Bitters Bottles*. Thomas Nelson and Sons: New York.